Essays From The Universe Experiencing Itself

Essays From The Universe Experiencing Itself

Edited by

Knujon Mapson and Amy Perry

A Pandeism Anthology Project Publication

CONTENTS

CONTENTS (cont.)

To Mom.

All Moms.

Preface

There is some tension inherent in the concept of a spiritual model which is claimed to be a natural thing, and yet at the same time claimed to be logical and the product of reason. For isn't nature unreasoning? Isn't the sprawl of vines and flowers the opposite of a product of rational thought? That is what our initial impression may be, and yet there is method to the chaos of nature. There is a mathematical underpinning to the structuring of cells and the development of organisms. There is reason and logic guiding the unfolding of nature.

And within that framework there is a natural place for a spirituality arising from reasoned and logical examination of the world. Across this volume, we will see examinations of Pandeism from a multitude of perspectives, and examinations of multiple perspectives which touch upon Pandeism as amongst a family of ideas yielding hopeful possibilities for the progress of spiritual knowledge.

David W. Bradford injects a dose of paganism as a key to unlock the shackles of religious formalism. After a refreshing does of spiritual optimism from Nichole Machen, entheogenic explorer Brian Graham relates the journeys that he has taken into the nature of our Universe, and camgirl legend Joey Kim provides a unique perspective on the rocky crossroads of religion and sexuality. Sridhar Venkateswaran indulges us with literary postmodernity, delving into the scientifically mapped destiny of our Universe.

Unitarian preacher C. Norman Myers reframes Jesus in terms more relatable to the times. Edward Vaughan Hyde Kenealy paints a poetic picture of a time that never was, nor could have been. Antonin Tuynman mulls the possibly pandeistically computational nature of it all, and Ewan Mochrie presents his unique theory of time. As always, our volume additionally is well set forth with poetic interludes.

It is our hope, as always, that every reader will find at least something to love and hold onto in this collection of essays, brought together with our blessings!!

Acknowledgments

The editors would like to acknowledge those who have been with us from the very beginning of our journey, and those who we have only come to know along the way. Antonin Tuynman returns a favor, as one of our authors contributed a piece to a recent anthology of his. Our literary agent Brian Abramson continues his fine work in keeping up with certain of our authors.

We are also deeply pleased to thank our superstar Kickstarter supporters:

Alex VIKOULOV
Nichole MACHEN
Alan H. DAWE
David W. BRADFORD
Cory BAKER
Gary ABRAMSON

Patterns

By Amy Perry

Amy Perry is a transcendental poet from California, United States. She has been featured in *Pandeism: An Anthology* and has graduated to co-editor of this second volume. Although writing is her greatest passion, she also enjoys gardening, cooking, yoga, learning, and good conversation. She enjoys experiencing life as a poem and invites you to do the same.

Life may seem
Complicated,
Requiring one
Most High,
But so much of it
Hinges on
Familiar patterns.
Follow the
Fibonacci sequence
Back to Source.
Find divine blueprints
On nautilus shells.
See how the Vesica Piscis
Represents the feminine.
See patterns in everything.
Fingerprints and clues
Riddled about the universe
Showing us wisdom and order
Exist amongst the chaos.

The Promising Path of Pandeistic Paganism, Or Having Your Spiritual Cake and Eating It Too!

By David W. Bradford

Once upon a time, in Pasadena, California, David W. Bradford was a professional photographer and artist, way back in the ancient mid 90's. The evil Adobe kraken twins, Photoshop and Illustrator, rendered much of his chemical photography and traditional art skills obsolete. This intrepid pirate then wandered off into the nerdy waters of information technology, and became a principal software developer. In 2019, he returned to his creative roots, and is again a studio and fine art photographer, as well as a relationship writer and aspiring novelist. He also paints, mostly with acrylic and mixed media. At heart he's a pirate, in the romantic and swashbuckling spirit, as well as still a tech nerd and definitive old school spooky goth.

"I believe in God, but not as one thing, not as an old man in the sky. I believe that what people call God is something in all of us. I believe that what Jesus and Mohammed and Buddha and all the rest said was right. It's just that the translations have gone wrong."
— John Lennon

● ● ● ●

In the beginning, humanity created the gods and the spirits... or so the story goes. Primitive people looked out into the world and saw many things that confused and scared them, so they attributed unseen qualities to what was around them, creating the first "spirits" of nature. This philosophy, called *animism*, was the first spirituality humanity embraced at a time when we still hunted large animals as hunter-gatherers, and still hadn't adopted agrarian farming practices — to largely brew beer, the true foundation of civilization.

In time, these spirits became gods, and these gods were all too human: vain gods, benevolent gods, cruel gods, foolish gods. All were attributed dominion over the uncontrollable aspects of the world and life. These gods became pantheons of deities, and changed as cultures grew and fell... as well as evolved into other cultures. Much of the stories of these deities appeared in the earliest writings, their stories evolved into parables and later "teachings." We'd invented the first revealed religions, where the laws of the gods were laid out, codified, written and those that opposed a specific *Word of God*™ were wrong and worthy of punishment and death. Sadly, humanity still hasn't grown out of this arrogance.

————

For many spirituality is a shackle, and for others a release. Nearly all of our holidays and festivals have ancient roots in old pagan holy days, celebrating the wheel of the year, the change of the seasons and the events of the gods. Modern day Christmas's date corresponds to the birth of the Zoroastrian sun god Mithra, a competing religion back in early Roman days with Christianity. Easter derives from the early Germanic goddess Ēostre and her spring equinox fertility festival. Trees, boughs of holly, candles, flowers, rabbits, eggs, crops and harvest are all inclusions of older pagan festival celebrations. But in reality, we as human beings need reasons to celebrate. The drudge of education, work, exercise, taxes and seeing the ugly things people do to one another can truly take its toll on us. Looking forward to a barbecue, large family dinner or simply dressing up as a sexy superhero for a holiday party can add a bit of zest to an otherwise monotonous existence.

Spirituality can add a source of personal power in an otherwise powerless life. Relying on a source of strength, hope and inspiration can truly help when we are struggling. The ancient gods and spirits represented archetypes and energies – feeling lonely, appeal to a love goddess; feeling weak, appeal to a courageous hero; feeling poor, appeal to a prosperity saint. Wearing a symbol, sigil or mandala associated with one of these archetypal sources of power became an amulet for them, despite the fact that we are the source of that power and it's the belief in that which shapes our actions.

But what is the nature of the divine? Is it entirely a creation of humanity or is there something to it? I'm a firm adherent of evolution, as it's beyond a belief: vestigial organs and reflexes, goosebumps echoing back to when our mammalian ancestors had fur, and the fact that our second chromosome possesses the split denoting our clading off from the rest of our fellow great apes are just some of the absolute proof of the common ancestry of life on our planet. Strong adherents of many revealed religions are resistant, if not combative, about accepting a human origin story that is not inscribed in the words of their own dogma, but our genetic code sings our true epic in undeniable prose.

When younger, I was very much a theist, that is believing in the concept of a personal divine. I wanted to feel as though there was somebody upstairs that was making sure everything worked out well for me. I prayed, believing that my prayers would be answered, though usually that answer ended up being a no. In time I grew from a monotheistic (one god) view of divinity, to a polytheistic pagan (many deities) view. I loved exploring paganism, more correctly *neopaganism.* I studied, practiced and later taught about Wicca, druidism, shamanism, divination, pathworking, ritual construction and magick (the "k" to separate it from stage magic). I loved the trappings of pagan rites, adding a bit of spice to the more socially acceptable rituals of communion and prayer – plus you got cool new toys to play with! Celebrating the harvest, seasons and wheel of the year made spirituality fun and enjoyable, rather than a means to alleviate guilt and fear of a horrific afterlife punishment by a hypocritical "loving" deity. I read as much as I could about all the world mythologies, enjoying the amazing stories that they had to share.

I eventually came to the personal conclusion that the divine couldn't care less about me. I liken it to two sports fans praying to the divine for their sport team to win the next match, when in reality a divine spirit able to create the incomprehensibly large and vast universe we live in couldn't care less about our paltry desires. With an estimated two trillion galaxies in the observable universe, each having on average 100 billion stars, with those stars having possible planets that could have also evolved life in some form, thinking any deity no matter how omnipotent could care about the individual needs and wants of a single human, just one species of the nearly nine million on our little world, with a population of 7.53 billion humans... is beyond arrogant and naive. Put simply, we are insignificant in even the most inflated view of our place in the universe. The divine is most likely too busy smashing distant galaxies together at the moment. This view of a detached elder creator spirit is the essence of a spiritual philosophy called *deism*.

I attempted to be an atheist for many years, since my love of science made it initially easy. After a few years, I was starting to question that line of reasoning. There are many things that are weird and amazing about our universe. The nature of evolution seems to be more of tinkering, rather than a celestially divine plan, but some truly beautiful things have evolved. The intricacies of the dance of sub-atomic particles mirror the celestial interplay of cosmic objects. There almost seems to be a plan, though very remote and subtle. There are those weird personal experiences, when you think about someone and out of the blue they call or message you despite not having talked in a while. Those moments where you are convinced something else is in the room with you while you are alone. When in a conversation someone completes your sentence or says the exact same thing you where going to. Also, there are those moments where everything seems like you are being looked out for, as significant streaks of luck occur in your life. There seems to be a little magick in the world, not contained in the laboratories of science. Meaningful coincidences, labeled *synchronicity* by the psychologist Carl Jung, can happen at a much higher rate that statistically likely.

What if I'd missed an obvious connection here? Why couldn't evolution and the big bang exist with a dispassionate creator spirit? What if on some subtle level of existence beyond our own, a spiritual energy of some form coalesced into a point of physical reality, and expanded and an incredible rate, creating particles, energy, basic elements and the first stars? What if this spirit sought to grow in some transcendent way, with the stellar explosions of those first stars causing the atomic fusion that created heavier elements to create clouds of stardust that would later collapse into planets, so this spirit could grow and evolve itself? What if this impetus of growth caused the first protein molecules to chain together and self replicate, later to form protective molecular shells and evolve into living single cell life forms. What if the universe, evolution and life are merely the expression of this growth, from a subtler level of reality for an ancient spirit to know itself? What if the only true word of god is etched in the laws of gravity, electro-magnetism and nuclear attraction? This is the heart of *pandeism,* that everything is divine and everything is connected, but we are nothing but infinitesimally small components of that non-personal divine spirit.

But this doesn't have to be a depressing thought. If we are part of the divine, then we have part of the divine nature. We can create, as well as preserve and destroy. Every piece of music is a creation. Every poem, every written word, or even turn of a phrase is a piece of creative divine magick. It was with this understanding that I realized that the philosophy of pandeism could blend quite beautifully with paganism, also known as *pandeistic paganism.*

The simplest definition of pandeistic paganism, is essentially having all religions and none, accepting the potential of all spiritually, without adhering to a personal concept of the divine. The acceptance that all spirituality is created by humanity in an attempt to understand existence, and that evolution and physics are the mechanics of that existence is a remarkable blending of magick and science. We can embrace kinship with all life on this planet, and that everything is inherently sacred as it's part of the divine, but also quite mundane as it's part of the universe. This allows us to pick and choose from all of the world's spiritual cultures to find a path that defines us, for whatever purpose we wish. By adopting a *catma*, instead of a dogma, we can have something independent, personal to our needs and which instills a great deal of enjoyment. To give an example, I'll share my personal approach to pandeistic paganism. Again, this is my own personal take. Feel free to borrow from it, but I have no interested in mandating it for anyone else.

Personal morality is really quite simple, and I pattern it off of a simplified Wiccan rede: *Do as you wish as long as it's not hurting others*. Many religions limit the food you eat, the sexual intimacies you can enjoy and even the words and thoughts you are allowed to have. In modern day settings, these are more means of controlling adherents, via guilt and a need for absolution simply because you are human. Some will ascribe immorality to the eating of certain meat and animal products, but it is very possible to eat meat in a reasonably cruelty-free manner if you are willing to research what you eat and how it is cared for in life. Personally, I only eat fowl and seafood, due to environment and cruelty considerations, cholesterol concerns and nutritional content — but I often chose the newer vegan meat replacements too. Sexual activity between consenting adults is not wrong, despite some believing that their own personal discomfort of thinking about how, and whom with, others couple should determine what intimacy should be against their laws. This world could definitely use more love and definitely is in need of better sex. When it comes down to it, if you basically try not to be a jerk to others by your actions, respect and ask for consent in your more personal dealings and try to make the world a better place for the rest of us, you have a better moral base than many who claim to be devoutly devoted to their divine.

I celebrate all the spirits. Across the world there are many sources of power to tap. I don't believe these to be intercessory or inherent divine, but they represent archetypal concepts that I may wish to embrace from time to time. Calling on the memory of a beloved ancestor, the strength of a mythological deity or even the passionate nature of an animal spirit can imbue a sense of change within you, whether only as a placebo or calling on possibly some of that mysterious cosmic power. Who really knows, but it can be enjoyable and it'll personalize your purpose for celebrating the year. I perform entertaining little rites for the full moons, the equinoxes and solstices and the mid points in between, such as May Day and Halloween. I celebrate traditional holidays such as Easter and Christmas, and culturally contrived ones such as International Talk Like A Pirate Day (September 19th) and Star Wars Day (May 5th). The point is to have fun with it, and make the year enjoyable, with silly moments to look forward to. Hey, it's my party, I can *wry* if want to.

I believe in a more organic form of reincarnation and karma. I believe in the butterfly effect, in that small actions cause greater impact globally in time. A smile I share with someone in a down mood can have incalculable effect as their lifted spirit can be transferred to others exponentially. Be cruel, and it has the same effect but in the negative. As for the nature of the spirit after life, I liken it to the fact that in any reaction, energy is neither created, nor destroyed, but merely changed. So what of the spiritual energy of the soul? Do I believe in a past life I was someone famous like Marie Antoinette or Alexander the Great... no. I don't believe our soul, if it truly exists, goes on complete to any one future person. Everything recirculates in this universe. Heck, the oxygen we are breathing once was in the prehistoric lungs of a dinosaur. What I believe is that I have some part of the souls of others from the past, so maybe not someone famous, but maybe it was John Henderson, frontier blacksmith... or maybe Agnes Smith, scullery maid? I hope I'm taking good care of their legacies.

I pattern the forces of change after mathematics and physics. The concept of sacred numbers and geometries have been used since the first humans could count on their fingers. These formed *microcosms*, conceptual ideas that pattern the greater world and universe, or *macrocosm*. I have a preference for threes, based on the primary forces of *creation*, *preservation* and *destruction*. Many take on a dualistic view of good vs. bad, us vs. them, left vs. right which inherently forces views to strong binary positions of opposition and conflict. I like the balance of three with *triplicity* (or *triality*) that is inherent in older spiritual beliefs, such as the maiden-mother-crone goddess concept, along with Western alchemical energies, Vedic gunas, etc. I also like other prime number microcosms, such as the five elements of Western and Eastern philosophies as well as the seven levels of chakras, early known planets or levels of the Kabbalistic tree of life. The associations of all of these can become symbols to focus on for meditation and introspection. Association is the heart of mysticism, and taking control and directing those associations to change yourself is the core of sympathetic magick. Does it matter, really, if it's scientifically proven, so long as you feel you have a bit of control in your life and it gives you a means of personal power? Psychologically speaking, a little optimistic delusion can be very helpful in a rather drab existential existence. If it works, why not? If not, at least you enjoyed the process.

The idea of the one true religion is common among the vast majority of religions. Amazing how all of the many branches of all those many religions, as they formed different sects and denominations, and grew, dare I say evolved, into different views on spirituality... incredibly make the one true religion the one that is prevalent in the geographical place you just happened to be born in? Spirituality doesn't have to be a bland meal plan when there's a bountiful buffet to choose from.

I choose to live, love and laugh in my spiritual life, with a little magick thrown in for spice... and to just sleep late on Sundays when I can. We all have the divine within us, so make up your own rules. I can guarantee you aren't going to Hell, Heck or Hades when you die, so why live there in life?

---- ---- ---- ----

And Just Like That

By Amy Perry

The Universe
Became itself
To experience
Itself,
Experiencing
Itself.

Taoist/Pandeist Alarm Clock

By John Ross, Jr.

John Ross, Jr. holds an ALM degree in Dramatic Arts from Harvard and two theological degrees: one from Boston University (S.T.M., Systematic Theology) and a second from Loyola University Chicago (M.P.S. Pastoral/*Religious Communication). John is the author of three science-religion poetry collections: Where the Designer Came From: Evolution, Creation, Hominids and the Skirmish of the Double Helix*, 2011; *COSMOTRINITY: Newton, Einstein, Hawking with the Origins of the Anthropic Principle and a Curtsy Toward QEDEM (Time)*, 2013; and more recently, *GENES, GERMS, GEODES and GOD: Verses Exploring Science, Faith, Doubt and Religion*, 2016. He is a senior lecturer in Theatre and Communication at Northeastern Illinois University in Chicago. He teaches courses in Drama, Leadership, Interpersonal Communication; and a new course entitled: "Communicating Science and Religion" based upon his new textbook: *SCIENCE & RELIGION: A Handbook for Interpersonal Dialogue, Discussion and Debate*, 2017. His academic interests surround the intersection between religion, science and the arts. He is currently finishing his Doctor of Ministry degree (D.Min) in *Transformational Leadership* at the Boston University School of Theology.

HOMO sapiens sapiens may sit and sport at chess 'til their alarm

Clock… *Drops* and charms …then…*Rocks.*

IT cushion-ticks *and* tocks: all *jade-eared* as tabled by the
yellow tides.

THEY wholly know their checkered Truth, those majestic
seconds by China's-told-times.

WE never quite comprehend their cost of a Rook, a Pawn, or a
dethroned Lady-Star Empress.

BUT let me tell you about the royal—younger *duo*, the high prince *Tao* and his *Sister Pan-deist* Tall.

THEY'RE check-mates, on a checker board and double-squared: the ones enshrined within us…*dialing*…*dialing* ever a call.

INVITING us as royals all!

For Bulls coach, God is no game (excerpt)

By Phil Jackson

Excerpt from "For Bulls coach, God is no game," then-Chicago Bulls head coach Phil Jackson interviewed on religion by sportswriter Michael Hirsley of the *Chicago Tribune*, April 27 1990, Section 2, Page 8. This is the seminal and ultimate quote of the piece, spaced for effect.

"I've always liked the concept

of God being

beyond anything that the
human mind can conceive.

I think there is a
pantheistic-deistic-
American Indian
combination religion
out there for Americans.

That rings true to me."

Waking Up into Understanding: A Positive Vibration

By Nichole Machen

Nichole Machen is a Service Manager with Mercedes-Benz in Southern California, where she has co-developed and managed a highly successful division of the service department that performed minor maintenance repairs. More importantly, she lives her life as a journey of discovery. She attended Fullerton JC and Whittier College – where her favorite course was a religious studies course – and she loves to live, dance, and travel. She can be found on Instagram documenting her milestones at @nicholem2727.

It is incredible how much of our existence we don't understand. If you think you have a clear understanding of how we exist in this world, I urge you to delve into the concept of quantum mechanics. I spend an inordinate amount of my free time going down the black hole (no pun intended) to learn about quantum physics and astrology. I believe understanding life begins with the understanding of life on the molecular level. It is incredible how learning about the complexities of life can make you feel so incredibly special and incredibly minuscule at the same time. Although I'm sure most people do not want to spend their free time learning about quantum theories and Astrophysics, I can promise you that watching 30 minutes of how our consciousness creates our reality, will make you appreciate all the "reality" shows we know and love even more!

For most, our understanding of the infinite is nearly impossible to fully comprehend. But what unifies our human experience is that we all can feel the infinite, the Divine, but cannot define its exact identity or our actual connection to it. Religion is our way of identifying our feeling of the infinite. In that respect, no religion is incorrect to the individual that perceives its definition of the truth. Our relationship and understanding of the Divine belongs purely to each of us individually. "If you do what you have always done, you will get what you have always gotten." I've come to a point in my life where I recognize the need to shift my perspective to develop a more powerful vision.

My moment of awakening occurred when I felt the connection with the universe. With my eyes now open, I am investing my time to understanding this connection and ultimately unlocking answers that will lead to my enlightenment. I share beliefs with Pandeism and believe that God became the entire universe and does not exist as a separate being from us. I believe that God is in all of us and we are all within Him. I have felt the connection with the Divine since I was very young, but could not fully accept the biblical version I was taught. I spent a lot of time studying the world's major religions and accepted many truths from each, but never fully adhered to one as my truth. It wasn't until I had begun to connect the many individual truths from various religions I had obtained, that I had begun to understand what I perceived to be God and that was the moment of my awakening.

As my understanding and knowledge of our Creator expands, I will be able to maintain a more fulfilled experience in this material reality and maximize my purpose while here. The truth I have discovered is that there is no pain that exists outside that which I manifest. My reality is not a byproduct of my circumstance, but a manifestation of all energies, beliefs and thoughts that I project into reality. Waking up is only the beginning. The phenomenon of "waking up" is quite literally an out of body experience. And there is a reason for that- it's because it is out of our physical form. You don't have to believe every word or even care to- but the message is clear. We have to put our faith back into humanity and live in love.

The world is waking up- we are beginning to receive the messages that are being sent to us. Your thoughts and emotions are more than internal feelings, they are contributing to the feelings of the world. Live in LOVE. Not only for yourself, but for humanity. Our connection to the higher power is stronger than it has ever been.

Learning how to tap into your natural born power begins with learning how to eliminate the social programming that mutes our connection to the Divine. I have never felt more connected to a message or information in my life. I have always been searching for something... knowledge or answers to questions that I'm not even conscious of having.

These ideas and concepts grab my attention and I'll stop and glimpse for a while, recognizing my attraction to the information but not understanding what it is or what to do with it. There is nothing more interesting to me than exploring the connection between humankind and the Divine. Something about indulging understanding into something we will never truly understand is intriguing to me. I feel that by investing in the meaning of our connection to our surroundings, we can improve on our relationships.

Some people have come into my life to make a positive impact; others have been in my life to teach me a lesson. Whatever our interaction (good or bad) - Know that I appreciate you. I am on a journey of discovering my truths and purpose in this life -- I see a long road ahead of me before I truly am enlightened, but I am extremely proud of how my mind and energy have evolved. --- The most incredible shift has been in my ability to recognize a person's negative opinions about myself (or others) as a reflection of their own insecurities.

I extend to each of you, this advice:

When you find yourself casting a negative judgment towards another person, ask yourself why *you* feel negatively about it. Assuming the person is not impeding on the freedoms of another, your negative judgments are likely branching from inner insecurities. Although we cannot completely control the existence of negative opinions, we can control the way we interpret it before emitting more of the negativity back into the universe. The world looks much different when you choose to see it in the light of love. If you live your life in love, then live it to the fullest and never apologize for it. You are not a pushover because you choose forgiveness; you are not clown because you choose to laugh. Don't be ashamed at how easily you live in the vibration of love. Some people will never know the feeling of effortless affection and positivity. That is one of life's greatest tragedies. Vibrate higher.

Stay Positive, friends.
You are the stars, the moon, the plants, the air.
You are everything and everything is you.

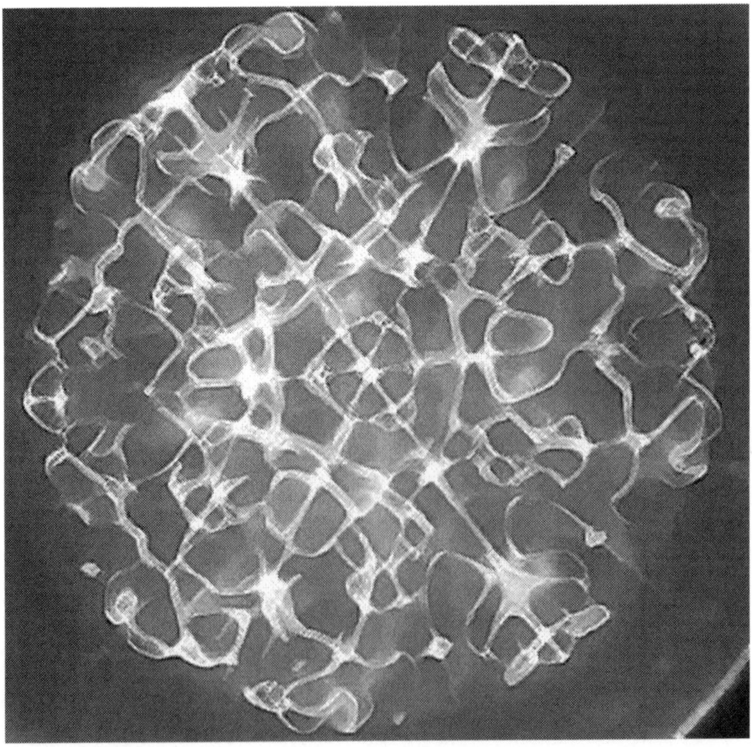

An Entheogenic Exploration of Pandeistic (Seeming) Experiences

By Brian Graham

Brian Graham is a contributor to his online journal, "A World Out of Mind" found on salviaspace.blogspot.com. In his writings, Graham explores consciousness and the ultimate nature of reality by intentional alteration of his own belief structures. To achieve these results, he uses *Salvia Divinorum* and additional self-altering meditational techniques drawn from Western ceremonial magic. You can also follow him on Twitter at @AWorldOutOfMind.

My First Experience with Salvia Divinorum

As a child, I remember going to sleep at night and staring at the ceiling, thinking that there must be more to this world than meets the eye. I'd visualize the stars above my house and wonder what lay beyond them. Every single night I would fall asleep with a sense of yearning for something, for some idea of what all of this means. As I grew up, over the years, I found myself drawn to books that offered at least some limited explanation of this reality, so naturally I gravitated toward the sciences, mostly biology and physics. I never did become a scientist, but I did learn that the scientific method is the very best way in which to question most anything. This, I think more than most factors, shaped my growing mind. I saw the value of that method in cutting through self-deception and false expectations. I applied this modality of thought to my Catholic upbringing and it's dogmatic answers to my Important Questions, and immediately found it sadly lacking.

I eventually came to the realization that there are two kinds of people in this world: those who believe and those who reason, and I was firmly ensconced in the latter camp. By this I mean that I needed to question everything, even myself, because I was getting some understanding of the fact that we humans are very flawed beings, and any one of us can be wrong about anything at any time. I observed that believers seemed to lack the ability to question themselves; in point of fact on many important matters they are explicitly forbidden to do so by the dogma of their religion. This is against my nature. I question everything, especially myself.

So I became an agnostic. I sometimes call myself an atheist, but only because I cannot bring myself to believe in a Theos, in an anthropomorphic creator deity. Forces and fields, sure, but not a God as it were. Agnostic is a better term, because I strongly felt that logically we cannot be absolutely sure that there is no God, no matter how much our scientific observations seem to contraindicate the need for one. I suppose I remain one to this day, at least in the sense of not being able to believe in a deity as most religions think of one, but I still have hope; not that there is a God, but that there is meaning.

As I grew up, my curiosity about the Universe and reality never waned. As I said, I had no "God-Shaped Hole" in my heart, but I hoped that there was more to reality than a Billiard-Ball Universe with only forces and fields, a cold, dead reality with no deeper meaning to it, however all I had was the hope. Whatever else I was looking for, it wasn't a religion. I was not to be deluded by my religion, nor by any of the other various faiths and cults and dogmas. All were equally invalid to me, and many seemed harmful, and frankly still do. I suppose I had formed myself into a materialist, or perhaps a scientific realist. Certainly, I was a person that dismissed anything that smacked of mysticism or the supernatural as very highly unlikely to be true.

Then in my thirties I had a series of unusual events happen to me, starting with a lucid dream which precipitated a long series of synchronistic coincidences in my life. The power and force of those coincidences eventually drove me to consider the possibility that maybe not all answers can be found in the current materialistic/scientific paradigm. The more that I read of quantum physics and various experiments involving solitary particles and the more I investigated various forms of mysticism, the more I opened my mind to more exotic possibilities, such as the idea that thought itself might have a role in reality; even that thought or consciousness in some form could be the very ground of all reality. At any rate, I had developed a strong intuition that "there's more to this sorry place than meets the eye" and I couldn't resolve it.

So that, more or less, was who I was and where I was at when I first tried Salvia Divinorum. It was an appropriate time of my life to encounter it. My wife heard of Salvia Divinorum from reading a news report about a celebrity who had claimed to be smoking it when a picture of her was taken that showed her with a water pipe. We looked it up on the Internet and found out that it was an hallucinogen and was legal. Legal? Really? Out of a perverse curiosity we ordered some online. It's legal; why not try it? I'd always been curious to try meditation with an hallucinogen to enhance the experience. So here was a legal one. How bad can it be? Simple as that.

We researched it online and found many warnings that one needed to have a "sitter" during the experience, so powerful was the effect; and yet some people apparently do not even feel any effect at all. How convenient. We mostly dismissed all of the talk about how powerful it was as likely to be simply exaggeration or hype; however it still seemed worth a try, once again because it was legal. My wife was on board with it, so I had my live-in "sitter." Which turned out to be a good thing.

The 35X salvia arrived in the mail, and that very night I resolved to try it. That evening my wife and I were in our bedroom, and I set up the apparatus. I had chosen a water pipe and a torch type butane lighter. I'd decided that smoking it was my best shot at actually feeling anything from it, since my reading had indicated that smoking an extract was far more powerful than either chewing or smoking the plain leaf. I half-filled the small bowl with powdered salvia divinorum leaf, enhanced with salvia extract to what is termed 35X, or thirty-five times the potency of the plain, unenhanced leaf. With my wife at my side, I sat on the edge of the bed, and inhaling as I did so, flamed the bowl. The powder vaporized in a very bright and hot flame.

What I was expecting, was somewhere between nothing at all, and perhaps some tingly sensation, or at most mild visual effects. What happened next changed my entire outlook on life.

I inhaled, holding the smoke deep in my lungs. I held my breath for perhaps twenty seconds, then exhaled. And then I honestly thought that I was having a stroke. Strong sensations of fast-traveling numbness throughout my body, along with a dimming of my eyesight with radiating concentric green and red visual effects like one has when one holds their breath too long. A tingling feeling as if there was a strong electric current running through me. I had the brief thought that I was having some violent reaction to something toxic, and that I'd better make peace with the idea that I was in the process of dying. However, I didn't have much time to contemplate my mortality for in the next instant, the far wall decided to rush me. It came at me like a freight train and absorbed me. I had no body. I didn't even recall ever having one, for that matter. I felt like I was a disembodied point of view in an infinite cavern of moving bands and indescribable shapes of intense rippling color, with something like a vast wheel or maybe more like a gigantic Rolodex near me, flipping through sheets that passed through me one after the other. I had the strong impression that these were universes, if that makes any sense. This lasted for what seemed like an hour, with many variations that I can no longer recall.

Then some "body sense" returned but I next found myself suspended in space bent over backwards, helpless, in that cavern of moving colors. I could not move. I felt the strong sensation of deja-vu throughout this experience. I'd been here before. After what seemed like another half-hour it all changed suddenly to a scene of a vast mountain, a huge mass, but made of beings somehow, or perhaps of the thoughts of many beings all massed together. A mountain of consciousness. I was physically imbedded in the side of this mountain, and I knew somehow that I could not ever get out of it, that I was a permanent part of it, like some barnacle stuck to a rock. It was as if the top of my body stuck out, but the bottom part from the waist down, was somehow integrated into this huge mass of consciousness, involved with it as a component of it.

I thought that I had died, and that this was the afterlife. (I'm still not sure that it wasn't!) I had this odd thought that I needed to wait for my parents to come and get me out of it. However, the parents that I thought of did not seem to me to be my actual parents that I grew up with. I also had this very strong sense of what can only be called nostalgia; I'd been here before, but a very long time ago, and my real parents would surely find me here eventually. And throughout this entire experience, there was this quality of actuality, of rightness, of this experience being more real than my regular waking life. It was my regular life that was the dream, not this; this cannot be doubted. But this was horrible! Was I really some sessile blob of consciousness stuck in a mass of other consciousnesses, only dreaming that I had a life in a reality where I was mobile and an individual? How very disturbing!

I slowly came out of it, returning to a jittery consciousness, and opened my eyes to see my wife in full panic mode. She told me that I'd taken the salvia, said "Oh God," and then froze. She had thought that I was joking until I started to drool. Relief didn't begin to describe her feelings as I finally came back to myself. Total elapsed time, perhaps twenty minutes. Just about ten minutes before my wife was planning to call 9-1-1. Yes, she was that panicked, and I can't say that I blame her.

The first thing that I said to her was "Get that stuff out of this house; it's evil!" I was shaken to the core. It had been a very difficult experience, one that I hadn't even been sure that I would survive. Almost a psychic rape. Then I thought about it. There was something about it that sparked my curiosity. The sensation of familiarity. The feeling that I'd been there before, even that that was my natural state somehow. The very strong sensation that it was somehow more real than my waking life. No, despite my initial reaction of strong aversion, I needed to explore this more. There were things to be learned here.

My subsequent experiences on salvia were far less disturbing. I'd been warned. I'd even been slapped. This was not just some drug that gave you a buzz, or made you feel silly, no, this was much more than a mere drug. This was a doorway. I've never felt anything like it. It leaves me awestruck every single time. I respect it as I do no other substance. It has the feel of a sacrament somehow, and I'm not even religious.

I started experimenting with lower dosages of the extract, even plain leaf, to ease myself into salvia space, for lack of a better term, rather than diving in with both feet. Over the subsequent three years I've partaken of it regularly, almost every evening. It's a relatively short experience, but always a very profound one. I learned that lower dosages left me with more control but still often produced interesting effects, often with me still conscious of my surroundings, so at first I confined myself to those, but after a while I strengthened the dosage to once again be immersed totally and completely in the bizarre world that is salvia space. And once I had some control of even those immersive experiences, which did not come easily, I began to really enjoy them. And those deeper experiences had much to teach me.

One is never prepared for that first experience of salvia. It comes at you from a direction that you are not aware exists. It takes you forcibly and suddenly and throws your entire consciousness into a blender, before you even can realize that you're starting to feel it. Many different kinds of experiences are possible, but there are some common themes, which I will discuss later. With a lot of practice one can in effect partition one's mind so that one retains a measure of waking awareness through some of the experience, but one thing is clear: Much of each experience does not come back with you. It's as if as you come out of salvia space, you have to pass through strata or layers of consciousness, and at each level memories of the experience that you just went through are stripped away. It is possible to carry one or perhaps even a few memories back with you, again only with practice, but one is also aware that much more is lost than is remembered afterwards. It feels like some of the knowledge that is gained there, you are not allowed to return with. I can remember knowing things that completely changed my view of reality, making me want to shout it to the world, and then a moment later feeling the knowledge just leak out of me, leaving me with only the distinct memory of having known it, and yet nothing of what it actually was.

I had had some previous experience with altering my own consciousness through meditation, concentration and ritual which was of some value, and I knew how alcohol affected me, and had some experience with marijuana, but really, nothing prepared me for the intensity of salvia space. I have since read several experiences of others that were used to other hallucinogens such as psilocybin or

LSD, and then had tried salvia, and the consensus was that the salvia experience is far more immersive and intense, albeit much shorter. On LSD, you see things around you, alterations of existing things or visual illusions, but you are still in your body. Salvia rips you out of your body. You have no body. You can no longer see the real-world objects around you; you are wholly immersed in a very dynamic and profound dreamlike state. I'd personally prefer to think of it as a vision. It seems like a doorway to one's deepest level of awareness, and yes, even beyond that to an awareness of the underlying structure of reality. Of course, this may all be illusory; I never fool myself that what I am perceiving is definitely real. That's how you get religion. However, one thing is definite: It feels more real than anything in my regular day-to-day life does.

Think about that for a moment. The experience seems more real than your regular life does. So much so that in fact, it feels like you are witnessing Ultimate Reality, as if you are awakened from the dream that is your regular life, and finally can see reality as it actually is. And it's amazing.

In salvia space, one does not only see, one apprehends directly. You can see a shape in front of you, for instance, and at the same time feel it, as if it were made out of your body. In this manner, you can experience a very complex phenomena and grasp it intuitively by how it feels. The problem with that is two-fold. First, remembering it. That is a battle. But if you can recall it, the next difficulty is being able to describe it. Much of what you experience in salvia space we simply have no language for. It is quite literally indescribable in any language. The experience has almost nothing that you can compare it to. It is too complex and immersive. The mind is seemingly able to perceive in more dimensions than it normally can. In some instances, it seems that your normal mental state is divided into a plurality, more of a group mind than a solitary individual one. You will see that I frequently say things like "it feels like" or "it seemed like." This is not indicative of any inaccuracy or fuzziness on my part; rather it is instead due to the near-impossibility of describing these states.

The salvia space experience feels holy somehow, sacred, and also has a flavor of extreme antiquity to it. It is not like you are experiencing something new; it is an experience that feels as ancient as the dawn of time. It is an experience that you strongly feel like you've had many times before, even the very first time that you try it. At least I did, and have read that others have noticed this as well.

I should mention that I do not recommend salvia for everybody. It is a very profound experience that can hurt you if you are not prepared for it, and perhaps even if you are. I've seen people use it in videos posted to the Internet where they have come out of it screaming in terror. Some of the experiences that I've had while in salvia space I think would have had a very negative effect on people with a propensity for mental illness; I would even say that it should be avoided by anybody too attached to reality, if that makes any sense.

If you are determined to try it, don't do what I did; take it seriously and start with lower dosages. I'd recommend no stronger than 5X extract if you're smoking it. Take baby steps and explore it with caution; I had to learn to do that the hard way. And at least in the beginning, always have a sitter.

I should also say that from what I've learned, my experiences are not the norm in all instances. From what I've learned, while different people can and do have vastly different experiences on salvia, it seems that mine are more often than not atypical, although in many ways there are some commonalities to be found. Many users of salvia have, for instance, reported experiences wherein they meet with and communicate with other beings or other people. Others report visiting the realm of the dead, in one way or another. I have not directly met other beings or people in my visions, at least not clearly, nor have I met with anybody among the deceased. There have been times when I sensed someone else present or heard a voice not my own, or seen others at a distance or even briefly up close, but no meetings and discussions with anybody or anything have occurred.

I also have a lot of experiences wherein I am not unaware of my surroundings, and in those I have eyes-open visions overlaid upon and even interacting with my actual view of reality around me, such as my bedroom. It is in many of those type of visionary experiences that I have discovered the most interesting things about myself and my reality. From what I've read, others seem to not have many such experiences, and usually either report vague tingly feelings and such while remaining conscious, or total immersion in salvia space without any ability to perceive their actual surroundings at the same time.

I credit some of these differences to my having developed the ability to retain some control on salvia through sheer practice, and also perhaps to my having had hypnagogic hallucinatory experiences as a young child of about seven years of age, perhaps due to some epileptiform ailment that went undiagnosed. I had seizures, which were eventually attributed to an allergy to the family cat, which promptly disappeared. My parents basically took it to the pound, I later discovered. My parents didn't believe me when I told them that I had these very bizarre visions overlaying my regular sight of the world around me and credited it to an active imagination. I know differently, because frankly they terrified me, so they're etched indelibly on my memory. Not only that, but in reduced intensity, they persist to this day as spinning “starfields” that I see all the time, more noticeably in dim light, which I tend to ignore. I recently realized that my present salvia visions are very similar to these past hallucinations of mine, even to the predominant color scheme, which incidentally is generally in hues of green and red. So perhaps due to these things, my visions are atypical for the substance in some regards.

I am also quite relaxed in my language here; I speak of what happens and how it seems, how it feels, and draw seemingly definite conclusions from it, but these conclusions are not necessarily true or correct just because I have experienced them as such. I am not so proud as to assume that my experiences on a powerful hallucinatory drug reflect actual reality, although they well might and certainly seem to. You will note that I often speak as if they do, but I must here acknowledge that I have no proof of their veracity other than my own subjective experiences, and if there's one thing that I've learned in this life it's that anybody can be wrong no matter how certain they are that they're not, and oddly enough that it is those who are the most certain that they are not wrong that usually turn out to be.

So in my uncertainty, which is unavoidable considering how I gleaned this type of knowledge and how inherently unprovable it necessarily is, I find myself holding a dual worldview now, in that I must still trust in and adhere to science and materialism and must admit that they may well be right and these sort of perceptions taken from visions may well be totally invalid and only seem to point in certain directions, all the while still being compelled by curiosity to investigate this more consciousness-oriented view of reality in which these visions may be a clue to the very structure of creation. For the purposes of these discussions I will often speak of the experiences and my conclusions as if they are real and true, in full knowledge of the fact that there is no concrete, non-subjective way to prove it.

Meeting God

I was eyes-closed and way out there at the fringes of our universe, and felt Its presence, but it was like It *was* this universe, or this universe was inside It; It formed the barrier which separates and cordons off this place from the rest of the All, from the Mind Which Is All That There Is, which is needless to say a much better place. I could clearly sense that after I die, I would have to experience It in some way, because I would be passing through It, which would not be pleasant, to say the least. However I was not without hope because I also saw and sensed directly, as only a salvia-tripper can understand that It was like a growth on the much larger whole of creation, and since I could not die, I would eventually be able to get through It and in time, whatever that means in this context, get past It to the better place. The place of the glowing green light, I think. The All.

In 2017, I had two experiences, about two weeks apart. Both of these were incredibly profound and the latter one was fairly scary as well. Both were in a darkened room, with a bluish-green light source. I vary the color of the light source for different kinds of meditations now. In each, I basically met God personally. It. No wait, hear me out.

On the first night, sitting in meditation, a very large "being" for lack of a better word, approached me quickly from my left side. It was very large, perceivable through the walls and floor and ceiling of my room, like a glowing mountain-sized amoeba. I'd met something like this before. This time, the being grabbed me. What I mean by this is that it came at me and engulfed my body about halfway, so that I was partially embedded in it, stuck fast. I could not move. The left half of my body, the half that was embedded in it, painlessly dissolved into it so that I felt like I was partially-digested, almost. I was integrated into it somehow. I felt like I was a tiny fly half-stuck in amber.

Then the communication began. None of it verbal, all fast-moving pure concepts thrown into my mind, pure understanding without language. I could see what I truly was. This being was showing it to me. After all, I'd been asking for it my entire life. This experience reduced me to a mere thought in that being's mind, nothing of what I thought that I was, no real body, all false, all a dream. I was just a thought, a piece of information in this being's vast mind.

I could see myself, but what I saw was not a body, but a symbol. It reminded me of an Arabic numeral, the number seven (7) only was more ornate, with hitches or slight curves to the top, horizontal part. I was this symbol, and nothing more, not to this being. Along with my symbol, I suddenly saw many other such symbols and was made to understand that these were all the other people in the world. Also merely the thoughts of this being.

So I was not alone, this was not solipsism. This was worse. Even I didn't exist. Nobody exists. Not as anything more than this being's thoughts. And yet I was not dismayed. There was a beauty to this. At least I could understand it. Towards the end of this experience I asked the being, out loud "How do I know that you're real and not my imagination?" As I finished the question, in less than a second, my air conditioner started to whine loudly. On cue. Now, my air conditioner whines occasionally. However, not very often. So it was a bit scary and rather convincing that I got an auditory reply to my question.

And then it was over, except I still had that "embedded in another being" sense afterwards, which gradually faded over the next hour or so. It was incredibly profound and it left me with a very positive feeling. A sort of lasting euphoria. That persisted until two weeks later, when, in another meditation, the being returned, but now it was angry.

Again I was embedded, as before. This time, however, the being showed me clearly that It wanted me to stop meditating on salvia, forever. I mildly object to referring to "God" as "Him." I certainly never got any impression of gender. I was in no position to disagree at the time. It was like I was in the jaws of a tiger and it was telling me what to do to avoid being eaten. For that was the implication, that the being would simply stop me, by causing me to die, at that very moment. So I agreed. It released me.

Apparently I lied to it, because I decided not to stop. I haven't had any more experiences with the being since. Truly, it's been hard to trip at all since. It's like my mind refuses to succumb to the beginning of the experience so I remain lucid. My rational mind dominates me too much to trip. This added to my lack of desire to write about my experiences. I seem to be getting over it, though.

Please note that I still do not believe this. The interesting thing is though, when you are having these experiences, there can be no doubt. The doubt, at least for me, happens later, when I'm no longer under the influence of the substance. These are the same kind of things that mystics the world over have said about reality, and Buddhist Monks for that matter. Vedanta speaks of similar things as well; so, for that matter, has Deepak Chopra. Both Vedanta and the teachings of Chopra have been compared to Pandeism. So, many people have come to this same or very similar conclusion. Why?

Many would say that it's because it's true, and maybe somehow it is. However, I also think that could this be us simply experiencing our own mind, or maybe better to say a part of our own mind that we do not normally have much conscious experience of; the part of our mind that dreams up the "hallucination" that we all experience as regular life. The constructed hallucination that is based on our sensory input. Just because we construct an hallucination of the world does not mean that the world is not real. It may simply be the only way that we can experience a real world, through constructing an hallucination, an imaginary but consistent image of what our senses are telling our brain is "out there." So once again, no way to prove it means I cannot believe in it. I'm either retaining my sanity or dissing God.

The Darkest Interpretation Of Reality

On many trips I have found myself in a situation where I seem to just know things about the Universe. In many of these I have run across a dark interpretation of reality that I've never heard any of the New Age crowd talk about. Oh sure, I hear them talk about how All Is One and how great that is, and how we are all facets of the One that is All There Is, and when we die we return to that source, that loving source of all, and how mindblowingly wonderful that must be. I mean, it does sound pretty good. And I do get a strong sense that we are indeed all facets of the One Thing; that we are indeed all One.

The people that believe in such things generally say that the One separated into the Many in order to create the Universe and all within it. It was an act of love, so they claim. What else would it be? Famed science fiction writer Robert A. Heinlein wrote in one of his books, "God split himself into a myriad parts that he might have friends. This may not be true, but it sounds good—and is no sillier than any other theology." On my travels into salvia space, I heard something else. More accurately, I sensed it as if it had happened to me. The One did indeed separate into the Many, but that was no act of love. It was an act of desperation fueled by abject horror. The One went insane, you see.

The One was all that there was, the only single solitary thing in existence, and eventually after eons of that, it fractured into the Many in much the same manner that a schizophrenic descends into madness - out of sheer stark-raving terror. It was so lonely, so very lonely, and it could only hold dialogue with itself. More utterly alone than anything we humans can even begin to imagine. Utter terror, the darkness of madness, and the prospect of eternal fearful isolation drove it to fracture itself into many minds all desperately trying to cling to and believe that they really are individuals which are completely separate from each other and above all else, that they're really, definitely, positively not in actuality only one being.

Please, oh please, oh please, let's never, ever, ever let ourselves remember that we're really all just one solitary being, not that, not ever, never please never, anything but that.

The whole reason we're here is so that we don't have to be there. There with the One, there in that awful state of knowing full well that we are not we, we are instead I, and I am fucking lonely and afraid and absolutely mindlessly terrified of my reality as the only fucking being in all existence. Not just the only being, but the only *thing!* Hell, there *is* no existence, only me.

Anything but that, anything but that, anything but that. Worse than death is eternal solitude. Worse than death is not being the Many. Worse than death is being all that there is. We cling to this reality with all our might, because it is the balm that soothes our brow, the sanity that we lack in our natural state as The One Single Being with nothing to do but contemplate itself and go eternally fucking nuts because of it. God has multiple personality disorder, times infinity.

The first time this came to me it overwhelmed me. I actually cried for The One in pity, feeling it's awful pain, vividly sensing its despair and loneliness, and then terror struck me as I realized that it was myself that I was crying for, for I am it, and it is me, and we are/I am a royal fucking mess. Yes, we/I deserve pity if anyone does, but there's no one to pity me but me, no one else to turn to for comfort, and no way to deal with myself and what I really am and remain sane, other than to deny to myself that that's what I really am. I must live a lie or face my own insanity.

So that's what I've been doing, for pretty much eternity now. Reality is a by-product of my desperate need to distract myself. I am the subject and the object. Not nearly as much fun as being the Alpha and Omega, let me assure you. So the multitudes are all a self-inflicted wound to distract me from the fact that I am all there fucking is, and all there fucking ever will be, forever and ever, amen. Individuals of a certain introspective temperament such as myself seek oneness, never realizing that we are only here as individuals in the first place because we are fleeing it desperately. Maybe sometimes finding higher knowledge isn't such a good thing.

Stretching out the Spiritual Side

I want to make it plain that I do truly retain my rational side throughout these experiences. I think these experiences, had they happened to anybody else that did not prioritize remaining linked to reality and not succumbing to beliefs, would have been transformed by them, believed them, and become a believer in God, at least a Deity of sorts. I did not. I am not a true believer, at least not yet, even with incredibly realistic and profound experiences. Here's why.

Science tells us that each and every one of us constructs a "dream" that is literally our only waking reality, based on the data we receive from our senses. So when I see another person, what I'm really doing is interpreting sensory data in signal form from my optic nerves and *translating* that information into a dream-form of the person I'm looking at. We only think we directly see things, directly sense things, but science tells us that this is not the case. We construct a dream of reality and confuse it with actual reality, which none of us has ever truly directly seen. Same with all the other senses. Our mind has no "direct contact" with reality, other than a hyper-realistic dream we all construct representing it. So, this is science. Not mysticism. This is how we see reality: We actually don't. None of us do.

Taking this scientific fact into consideration, I think it is possible under deeply altered mental states produced by various means, including drugs and meditation, to become able to perceive that your reality is "nothing but a dream" and still be wrong. You may be merely perceiving the fact that, yes, reality is a dream to all of us, because that's how the brain processes sensory information, by constructing a dream to fit it. You may be perceiving the actual dream of reality in all of us, not some overarching dream reality in the mind of The One, or a Monad of some kind. We ourselves may be the Monad. Our own minds may be the culprits here. We may be merely perceiving our own World Dream, not an actual dream-based reality but a necessary evolved function of the normal mind required to integrate sensory information.

This would also neatly explain why so many people who use psychedelics and entheogens report that the experiences seemed "realer than real life." When you consider the fact that your "real life" is a constructed dream based on sensory information and you're looking under the surface of that constructed dream from an altered state that is more basic, closer to your inner self than your constructed dream is, of course it looks "less real." It is! We made it! At some level we realize it isn't real.

I also have had so many experiences in visions and meditations with salvia divinorum that have seemingly affected reality, from awakening my wife or dog on cue, to things like the air conditioner whining or other sounds perfectly on cue like that, that I must still remain neutral and uncommitted. Once I simply took my salvia, the "rush" hit me, and all the lights in the house went out for about four seconds. An actual power outage, rare here.

It seems that all is a dream, all is a constructed hallucination. That much I'm certain about. When I meet a deity in this hallucination, that deity is me, the me having the hallucination. A part of me that integrates with the rest of the world and translates sensory impressions into my reality-dream.

To define that demiurge being in the context of the I AM, I'd have to say that what I perceive is that there are consciousnesses greater than ours, much greater, and yet still not anywhere near the I AM. Other beings that swim in these seas, as it were. That was one of those.

Whereas the two beings in My Two Gods" seemed to *be* the *I AM*. Yet they were not consistent, one with the other! You see my quandary here. To summarize, it seems as likely that this could be all in my imagination, relating to my mind constructing a dreamlike hallucination based on sensory inputs, like everybody else does unknowingly.

OR

Or it could be that I'm sensing my Higher Self, which is also pretty much God, and is also everybody else's higher self. This is pandeism. If all of us are God at the core, then God is all.

OR

Or it could be that I'm alone in the universe and I imagine that everybody else exists due to my terrible loneliness. Solipsism.

To me, judging from how it *feels*, the third option seems most likely.

This reality we all see around us, isn't real. It's consciousness. A dreamlike state, only with rules. Now, I can see ways that that could fit into many theories about reality, from "all is mathematics" to "all is consciousness" to "all is ME." What does seem to be ruled out for me, is the basic scientific realism paradigm. the 'billiard-ball universe." No way that's real. I get far too many synchronicities for that. Too many reflections of my own mind in my reality around me.

Also, there are "combination options." How about the "All is Mathematics" taken to a different level? All is math, so consciousness is math, so math can be consciousness, so maybe math *is* a kind of consciousness, so maybe Math is God. Lately I'm also directly sensing, while meditating, that mathematics is involved in my own mental processes. I'm beginning to directly sense the mathematical nature of thought itself, so I think it's possible that mathematics, not consciousness per se, is the "ground of all being." As in, we're all literally "made of mathematics." Everything is math. However, what does this mean, if true? It means that all our most emotional experiences, even love, and all our most abstract thoughts and imaginings, are still "merely" a flowing, incredibly complex mathematical process. Such incredible complexity is to be expected when considering the vast spans of time involved in our development.

It means that all consciousness is a mathematical process. All consciousness is mathematics. Therefore, mathematics can be consciousness, or even conscious. Therefore, certain aspects of our mathematical reality can seem to be consciousness-based when they're really mathematics-based. What can you think of that would still remain if you eliminated space, time, matter, and energy? The only thing I can think of that quite possibly cannot *not* exist, is mathematics.

Science, specifically physics, tells us that the past is real. We can never journey to it, but the past, at least according to our best mathematics, is still "there" somehow. If we could go back in time, there would be time to go back to. Think of the implications. All our memories of the past, we're still "back there" making them. We're all still alive in the past, experiencing, perhaps over and over, those remembered experiences. If I could travel back to my past, I could see myself making the very memories that I carry of that time in my head.

When I die, science tells us that I will still be alive in my past. We are all still alive in our past timelines after we die. Quite literally, forever. Now, let's add in the concept of a multiverse, since this seems to cry out for one. If I die, but I'm still alive in the past, it is possible that I, or rather my consciousness, will merely, as I expire, return to a previous time that I can remember in my past. But then there would be two of my consciousnesses there. Or would there be?

What would likely happen would be a split, a divergence of universes, creating a new one in which I explore a different path. A different future. A different death. And the cycle continues. We'd all explore an infinity of paths forever. Literally forever. It sounds kind of nice. Certainly better than many religions. Do I believe it? You know the answer by now. At this point I would have told you that I'm not the best choice to support pandeism even though it jibes with some of my experiences. Really, I was closer to a solipsist! But I found the pandeism option to be as likely as any other. I wondered if I'd ever truly believe anything, ever again. Best not to, I think. Too dangerous.

2020

And after all of this, I had the clearest experience yet. Hard to describe the degree of certainty I felt during the experience, but I was reality-testing all the time, comparing it to my regular reality and I think this is *more real* as in an actual view of the underpinnings of things. I felt the world as my body, the truth of it, all is one, but more so, all is me and I am all and the world is my body. I saw the cycle of creation and how it folds back upon itself and purges and begins anew. The universe is my body and my view of the universe is me looking at myself. You are within me, and I am within you.

I talked to God again but realized it was me all along. And you. We all are part of it. I still don't like the word "god" by the way, but God didn't seem to mind. It was a very small voice within me, part of me all along. Drowned out by the louder voices and the chaos of my inner life. I was everything, so you aren't real. Yet, neither am I! That's the key. We think we're real in the sense of being separate individual beings but we really are just one being in many forms. Or rather in one form, a giant play, a composite dream. I didn't feel any zeal here, this time. No amazing emotions. I was cold inside, in the sense of shutting down my emotions so that they could not deceive me. I didn't care what God felt or if God got angry. Nope. (God being me all along, and you, etc.)

This started by me being in several separate planes at once, then *refusing to choose one* and forcing the vision to continue in a multi-mind state. Then my being just fucking expanded to include everything. I knew while in this vision that I would later be skeptical of what I was seeing, so I tried as much as possible to replicate my regular normal mindset in a sub-mind and use that version of me to test the reality of the vision, and it could not falsify any of it. Keep in mind here that it (I) was trying to use reason to falsify, but it (I) also was experiencing the vision and considering the nature and force of the vision, it could find no way to prioritize our waking reality over this new data set. The new data set provided by the vision was more realistic than regular life is. I mean, look around. It's not a very realistic reality we find ourselves in right now.

There's a difference in me today.

Today I no longer see my skin as the limits of my body.

I see everything and everybody as part of my actual body now. At a gut level.

It falters sometimes out of habit, but my last experience pretty much convinced me. I was even sending my later waking self the message that "I know you won't remember all the details of your vision last night but you have to trust me, if you could, you'd be convinced, and furthermore I wish I could make it so that you could remember it all, but you were using more than one mind to think that way. It's not possible in just one."

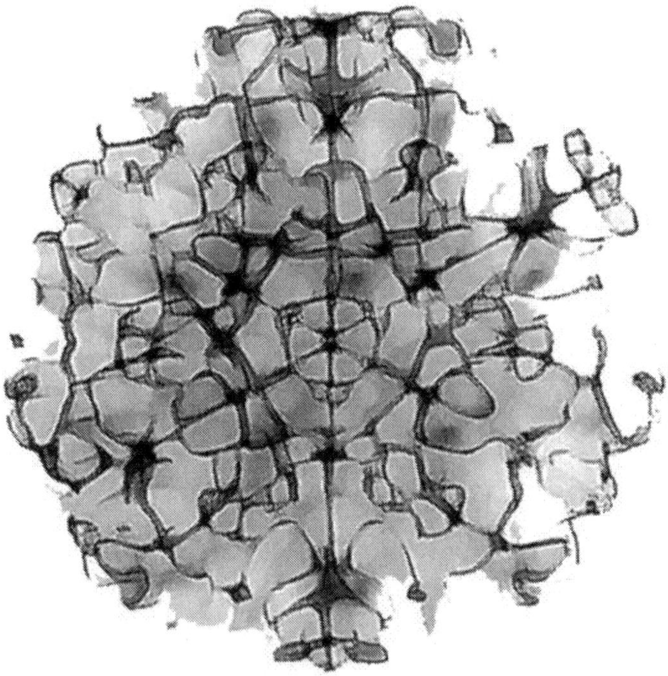

Simple Pandeism

By Amy Perry

It's easy
To overcomplicate
Things.
When discussing
The origins
Of the Universe
It's pretty easy
To feel
Overwhelmed,
Insignificant,
Out of place.
But you are
Just where you
Need to be.
Soaking it all in,
Absorbing experiences
Like the roots
Drink the rain.
Your eyes are
The vehicle
For universal
Understanding.
The sensory
Manifestations
You gather
Culminating into
Humanity's story,
Earth's poetry,
And Deus' art.
Feel it all, enflamed.
Write your story,
So it can be
All of our
Stories.

Spiritual Perspectives of A Wandering Sexual Artist

By Joey Kim

Joey Kim is a traveling dancer, performer, and webcam model. Kim debuted as a webcam model when she was a sophomore studying photography at Parsons School of Design in New York. With her photography experience, Kim creates captivating self-portraits and videos. Kim has twice been featured in *Penthouse*, is signed with Bespoke Talent Agency in New York, and is invited to perform at gatherings all over the world. You can find her at JoeyKim.tv.

© Joey Kim

She slept in the white light of the moon and a sky full of hand picked stars. There were no one there, just a tinge of moist air and her black and blue hair. She moved like a serpent. And the gaping space between her legs was her solitude. She placed herself in alien hands for direction, sleeping in a fever of dreams.[1]

I get naked for a living.

I get naked for a living.

I wanted to say that twice to make sure that it registers and that it's not an incidental footnote stuffed in a small corner in the bottom of a book or something that no one is ever going to see. While the conservative (i.e. "religious") right would call what I do sinful, and anti-pro-sex feminists look at me with pity, thinking that I'm a poor misguided soul seeking approval under the yoke of patriarchal powers, I remain fine with what I do and seek to be good at my job just in the same way any other person wishes to be good at their occupation.

I'm self-employed, I make my own hours, I earn my own money, I'm my own producer, and I am my own brand. If I were in another industry, I'd be considered successful, but that's not how society—and particularly its conventional religions, which are a distillation of societal mores—looks at what I do or people like me.[2]

Religion, Sexuality, and Shame

I do not fall into a single group of belief systems. I try to stay open minded to everyone's philosophy and keep what resonates with me.[3] I can resonate with some aspects of spirituality, satanism, Buddhism, and even Christianity. I can resonate with Pandeism, a philosophy which takes a different approach but still hits on certain of the more positive themes claimed by religions, like acting lovingly towards others.

But I am also none of these things.[4] I do not worship any god. I worship myself, in knowing that everything I need to reach my highest potential, is already all within me.[5] Some people will claim that I sold my soul to the devil when I chose my work. But in exchange I got my independence, freedom, strength, and fearlessness. I allowed the stigma and judgement to bring me to my darkest low, and only then did I begin to grow.[6] After all, if "God" punishes you for living happily, and for living the life you want, who is actually the devil?[7]

Before streaming, I did not understand in the power of the Universe. To be honest, I didn't even believe in one. Or the importance of self love. Since building all the friends I have today from streaming, the ladies and men who support and lift me up daily, I rediscovered my childlike awe, and wonderment. I've experienced a lot of ups and downs, but I feel a sense of peace that I never knew was possible.[8]

One of my favorite nude photo series, titled "Fallen Women," prominently features a statue of an angel. Angels were a common theme in Nineteenth century depictions of women in art, especially those of pre-Raphaelite artists. The poses of the models mimic those seen in classical sculpture. In another time period—for example, the time of Aristotle and Socrates—it was acceptable to depict female nudity in the name of art. During the Nineteenth century however, the time when the tombstones which appear as the backdrop for this photo series were built, female nudity was taboo.

The Victorians believed passion to be deviant, thoughts of sexuality would cause insanity and thus sexuality was to be repressed. Popular paintings by pre-Raphaelite artists and sculptures were of beautiful women, but women who suffered as a result of their insatiable sexuality. Women were "angels of the hearth," idealized as chaste and subservient to the needs of their family. The presence of angels presiding over the tombs of loved ones was not only a commentary of the deceased wife, daughter or sister's virtue, but also served as a didactic tool that reinforced the prevalent gender norms of the 19th century.[9]

In a world of political correctness, it is not nice to talk about religion if it might make atheists uncomfortable, and vice versa. It's a world of yellow elongated fruits, not bananas. But if we stop identifying reality, then we live in a fantasy land and, unfortunately, every person's fantasy will be different. So it's important to present people with the real face of real human sexuality. At this point, with open season on anyone or anything the religious right sees as 'abnormal'—that is, normal—it is essential to demystify female sexuality, and to present it as it is. If I am willing to do this, then I will have to accept that, until a critical mass of information is produced and a critical population of people have seen and accepted it, I will be subject to the fear-bases lashings out of a sexually repressed society.[10]

Beyond criticism of pornography itself, shame and suppression when talking about nudity and sexuality tells us it is immoral to act upon sexual desires. The battle between legalization of same-sex marriage, asserts to us that same-sex relationships are controversial or wrong. Female and male genders who discover romantic desires towards the same sex are taught to suppress them-including, those who identify with a separate sexual orientation than the body they are born in. Finding comfort under one's skin is not celebrated but I believe if celebrated, an open dialogue can happen dealing with a subject we all keep private.

This. Hurts. People.[11]

If you've spent much time on social media, you've probably at some point come across a graphic video of a few Middle Eastern men creating a female eunuch, that is, forcibly and without medical skills or tools, removing a twelve-year-old's clitoris. If you read the *New York Times* you've probably heard of the story of Tyler Clementi, an 18-year-old Rutgers University freshman who killed himself in September 2010 after discovering that his roommate had secretly used a webcam to stream Mr. Clementi's romantic interlude with another man over the Internet. Or a similar story on Amanda Todd a 15-year-old Canadian girl, whom after exposing her breasts via webcam committed suicide after suffering torment from cyber bullying that led to depression and anxiety.

Somewhere between those points is where most Americans would find themselves on the sexual shame scale. The young Middle Eastern girl wasn't ashamed, not before being mutilated. I'll bet that she is afterward. Why would huge men bind her and pin her down and cut out a part of her? A part she couldn't even really see, but probably, by then, knew was there. Possibly she even knew it was a source of pleasure. Now, forever and ever, it would be a source of pain. And shame. It would be the odd culture in which a pre-teen would be comfortable with several grown men seeing her maturing body, never mind cutting it to pieces.

Young girls and boys are learning every day that their sexuality and their bodies are shameful. But what about adults, male and female, who would be too embarrassed to even watch that horrific video, who avoid going to art galleries where sexuality is obviously part of the artist's statement?

A few years ago, an article on Salon.com suggested that sexual shame causes cancer. The author came to that conclusion because half of the women who have Pap smears never return for a second one, having found the experience of an often-male doctor too embarrassing to cope with again.

Sexual shame causes enormous suffering, even when it isn't accompanied by forcible sexual mutilation. Women spend enormous amounts on clothing and cosmetics in order to feel attractive. When they attract a man, it's a toss-up whether the man will think the woman is "frigid" if she fails to allow him access to her vagina when he decides it is time, or a whore if she allows him to penetrate when he wants to, or worse, invites him to do so.

What's a woman to do? Simple. Confront sexual shame where it lives. One way to do that is to create art that uses female bodies and bodily processes as essential elements.[12] By celebrating the beauty of the nude female form and the passion of its expression, my aforementioned

"Fallen Women" photo series juxtaposes and critiques the suppression of feminine sexuality, and it does so in the context of religious symbolism.[13] Another performance that I created is called "The Blood of Christ." Wine is symbolic of the blood of Christ. The Christian bible says:

> WHEN A WOMAN HAS A DISCHARGE, AND THE DISCHARGE IN HER BODY IS BLOOD, SHE SHALL BE IN HER MENSTRUAL IMPURITY FOR SEVEN DAYS, AND WHOEVER TOUCHES HER SHALL BE UNCLEAN UNTIL THE EVENING. AND EVERYTHING ON WHICH SHE LIES DURING HER MENSTRUAL IMPURITY SHALL BE UNCLEAN."[14]

The message is dangerous because they use their moral tone to demean all women and a woman's natural bodily functions. Dating back for centuries, the woman's menstrual period had always been a source of shame.

Once every month, my menstrual cycle will begin. As a woman growing up, the world always seemed to look at it with disdain, as something grotesque, or shameful. However, for women, it is our reality, and our body's natural way of cleansing itself in preparation to hold another life in its womb.

In light of one of the biggest Christian holidays, Christmas, I created a conceptual performance that shines a positive light towards menstruation. I drew parallels to the symbolism of Christ's blood, and the blood of menstruation. Wine is symbolic of Christ's blood, and similarly to the waning womb, it is symbolic of life, death, renewal, and of hope and rebirth.

I chose to begin my performance during the heaviest day of my menstrual cycle. It was important to me to document this performance using real menstruation blood to represent the authentic process of menstruation. A lot of men imagine period blood to fall freely out of a vagina like a fountain, but the women's cleansing of the womb is actually a week long process. I sat there patiently with the wine glass underneath me in a span of hours waiting for one drop of my blood to fall into the glass. Menstrual blood to me, symbolizes renewal, rebirth, and hope for life. The backlash over a woman's menstruation is about oppression of women. This performance aims to celebrate the beauty and magic of the female body.[15]

But there is also an element of ethics that enters the discussion at the point where the body is used for such artistic purposes. If an artist wishes to attack the creation of sexual shame in a society by making art that involves overt female sexuality, whose sexuality is she entitled to use? She could, of course, ask her friends to permit her to use their bodies. She could hire models.

In fact, hiring models is very basic to the creation of art, as it is necessary to see and know where human muscles and bones are in relation to each other. It is the rare model of either gender, however, who displays sexually active portions of their bodies except insofar as those areas are naturally exposed in an ordinary pose.

And therein lies another possibility for sexual shame, but usually on the part of the art students rather than the models. The models have decided, before the first class they pose for, that other people looking intently at their bodies and drawing all parts thereof is fine. Students? Not so much. When I was still a student in an art university, my professor had to repeat time and time again, "How can you draw the model if you don't look at the model? She doesn't mind, I promise. LOOK AT THE MODEL."

It is obvious that young Americans of college age—for no high school would dare in repressed America to offer life-drawing with nude models—are completely abashed by the thought of looking at a naked, usually female, human body. And this despite the fact that they spend a great deal of non-academic time figuring out how to get some sexual experience themselves.

The most ethical thing for an artist to do, then, is to use her own body as a subject for her work. This will open her to all sorts of unwanted attention, of course. She will be thought a whore for being an exhibitionist (the fact that there are Kardashians in the world notwithstanding.) She will be exempted to work in many other work fields. She will be verbally abused; those who are wildly conflicted about the place of sexuality in the universe and their own part in it will attempt to threaten her. Stalking is common for women artists and sex workers who create erotic, or even clinical, works using their own sexuality. While most artists and sex workers are treated to a modicum of disdain, at least until they become famous, a woman who uses her own body to create portraits displaying sexuality will be subject to all that in an astonishing degree.[16]

There is a lot of judgment, imposition of double standards and one-sided discussion on the issue of sex and the female body. Jayn Griffith said that when a woman is depicted in a sexualized way, with no depth to her appearance with the intent of selling beer, cars, food or when overtly sexual or nude photos, like the Kim Kardashian nude tweets, are posted online or printed in magazines, we call it objectification. Objectification, of course, has a negative connotation. I like to consider most objectification as self-objectification, considering that the women behind the image consensually or even passionately wanted to be captured in that image. Objectification is a term with negative connotations.

That seems strange but easy to follow, but it gets way more complicated. A model is still considered a legitimate perspective depending on who they are working for or what they are selling. A person selling sexuality, fantasy or themselves, however, is void of morality. Being a porn star is considered "incredibly shameful for a young woman."[17] While female porn stars should be looked upon with shame, when the young boy is caught looking at porn on the computer or with his dad's *Playboy*, we'll probably hear "Well, boys will be boys..." Go back to the equation; boys looking at porn is okay within reason because it's a natural part of sexual exploration. Girls providing porn, however, are sluts.[18]—even though a 2012 scientific study found that women who work in sexual fields report higher self-esteem and bonding with their spirituality.[19]

So I, the self-employed sex industry worker, am a slut that should be ashamed of myself.[20] This job came with so much judgement, and when I began camming, I was not prepared for it. Judgement from family, friends, total strangers. I used to cry alone reading people's comments about me. It hurt so much. But it built me up. It taught me I couldn't live for anyone else.[21] Rather than being some textbook equation that a couple guys in suits drew up in congress or the back room of a church, this is actually something that's easiest to see as an unspoken undercurrent and cultural attitude present in our society. I have a simple story to show how it looks in practice.[22]

Coming from an Asian family, my family has expectations of me to become a doctor or a lawyer. It hurt to go against that because I love them. But I only have one life.[23] Like many young people, I never wanted to disappoint my parents, who does? So you can understand my apprehension about telling my mother that I worked in the sex industry in a society where sex industry workers are marginalized. It's not exactly the thing you bring up at the PTA meeting. "Well my oldest daughter you see is a sex worker...." My mom has a rudimentary understanding of what I do but like most people who go to work every day, we don't walk our parents through how our days look. "I get up, I brush my teeth, I masturbate, and go to work, at 10 am I have a break, and at noon we have a meeting, then I do content editing blah blah blah," no one really has conversations like this so it shouldn't be a surprise my mom doesn't know exactly how my day looks. She's a woman, she's seen my websites and she's seen prints of my nude self-portraits. She's even been to a burlesque show where I stripped fully naked. My mom, therefore, is as supportive as I could ever want her to be, however, still I always feared my mom would hear about or see something about me doing "porn" on the internet and this could be the one thing she may not understand or could not be able to handle.

So when the phone rings and it's my mom, I naturally get nervous sometimes and recently, my worst fears were realized. Chatting with her college student neighbors, who are younger than myself, the young men informed my mom that they were on a website and they saw my porn online. Thankfully, my mother wasn't bothered by this, but I was. In fact, the implications of culture and society that are revealed from this little act say multitudes about double standards and gender norms in our society. Let's frame all the details from this particular story:

(1). male college students told my mom they were watching porn
(2). male college students told my mother they were watching her daughter do porn

This solicits a few logical questions. First, what was the intent of them telling her this? Were they attempting to warn her so she could "save" me, were they attempting to shame our family, or were they just having casual conversation? Let's rule out option three because we don't have casual conversations about watching pornography, having sex and/or masturbating, particularly with someone's mom. So, that means these boys, who were themselves watching porn (and perhaps viewing intellectual property illegally), either wanted to shame me to my mom or warn my mom so she could save me.

In their own culturally inundated and gender role inundated psyche, they saw nothing strange about telling my mom they were viewing pornographic images, but they felt it important enough to have an awkward conversation with her so they can either "help the poor porn star" or get on their high horse and "shame the porn star's family." Either way, it didn't work, but let's be honest, my mom probably is not the parental norm in such a situation. Had I been born in a different home this could have met losing my place to live, getting disowned by the family or under Sharif law—that same kind of law that has been used to justify the genital mutilation of little girls— this would be grounds for death. We have to identify these antiquated double standards and ask ourselves as a society what is the motivation other than control and subjugation behind these cultural artifacts.[24]

The duality in American culture regarding proper sexuality and improper sexuality is not only mind-boggling, but unworkable. It results in sexual misconduct, but mainly because sexual good conduct is so completely stifled and narrowly defined.

It would seem, if one is concerned about the fabric of society at all, that it is one's duty to confront sexual shame early and often. Not all artists will decide to take on that task; some will prefer to engage in experiments with color or form or mixed media or Peeps. Some will, however, decide that it will be impossible for society to actually see art properly until their eyes are opened to the totality of human experience, which includes sexuality.

Sexuality, being central to the human experience—indeed, there would not be a human experience without it—seems a fitting arena for artistic sexual exploration. Like color. Or form. Or media.

However, color, form and media do not carry huge burdens of loathing and fear; sexuality does. Just as Van Gogh is known mainly for cutting off his ear because his behavior was outside the mainstream of his society, so modern artists who work in sexual formats are likely to be known for that for some time to come, rather than for their work itself.[25]

Imagery of a nude body and public expression of sexuality provokes derogatory name-calling and hate speech. Inflicting shame does more harm than it aids people. The open expressions of sexuality have become in a way, the ability to break the cultural standards. In a sense I am objectifying myself. But in many ways my body, which is the subject of many of my art pieces, is an object of meaning. My body- the subject of a lot of my work, has become for me an object that harbors my weaknesses, my fears, but also my strengths.[26] I feel like masturbation is a great form of meditation. You really fall into the present moment and connect with your body, mind and heart.[27] I find that objectification when dealing with the nude body has negative connotations. There is a huge misconception that objectification of the body is objectification that happens without meaning.

Photographing myself has become a personal journey of self-acceptance, and self-reflection. Being comfortable in my body in the silence of my own home and photographing myself is not the hardest process of creating my photographs. The biggest struggle is the response of the public eye but learning to accept that this is why creating this work is so important and meaningful to me.[28]

A woman who creates erotic work using herself as a model will have to take her work as a mission in order to survive. She will need to dedicate herself to it not as art for art's sake or sex work for sex work sake, but as open sexual expression for society's sake as well.

She is likely to have her private information leaked; to those who fear sexuality, the fact that a person would paint her own breasts on a canvas, and display the resulting artwork to others, is the same as inviting the world to her bedroom. She is likely to be ostracized from certain groups. She may have her own family refuse to tell people what her work is; she may be prevented from babysitting the family's children, as if her sexuality and how she uses it had anything to do with caring properly for children. In short, the rampant confusion in American society resulting from its fear of female sexuality (although there is also some of male sexuality, although that most often has racial overtones, still, as well but would need an entirely new blog entry) results in all sorts of rending of the normal social fabric into one that is riddled with lumps, bumps and extrusions. A cancer of sorts, one might conclude, of the society itself.

Today, still, many women use their sexuality as an empowering economic advantage; others hide their sexuality so thoroughly that it is difficult to tell that they are women at all.

This is the truth: Ethical artists and sex workers interested in improving the social fabric will continue to bear the insults, the stalking, the threats and use their best material—their own body and their own body of knowledge—to display female sexuality in ways that cannot be ignored. Only when female sexuality is open to the entire society will the tendency to feel shame disappear, along with the tendency to engage in shaming others.[29] Because a world where we all saw each other as human with compassion, and understanding, deserving of love, kindness, and respect, regardless of occupation, gender, or ethnicity, would result a world with less violence, and less duality and separation. Is it wishful thinking?[30]

It is difficult. It is an extra step into the unknown that most artists don't have to contemplate, never mind take; artists and sex workers step off into one unknown or another every day they work. As an artist working in eroticism, especially one ethically using my own body as model, I need to be mentally strong, just as the freedom riders for legal equality of the races were. In the end, using art to change ignorance to acceptance to knowledge to celebration is not an easy task. Only when one requires no approval from outside themselves can they own themselves. But it is one artists of both deep perception and willingness to take bold and difficult steps are uniquely qualified to do.[31]

"If men can watch porn without judgment, then women have the right to make sex their career." - My mom.[32]

My Travels

Life is way too short to live within the confines of our comfort zones. I never wanted a traditional job or to be limited by societal norms. I always took risks and these risks have always changed my life for the better. Decisions both good and bad have made me the woman I am today and some of the biggest risks have been the most life changing. I always trust my intuition, which isn't always easy, sometimes it's scary or it might even seem crazy, but it the end it always made me a better person.

It is because of this outlook on life that, while travelling in Europe, I finally mustered up the courage to cancel my flight home. I understood then: I'm in a foreign country. I don't speak the language. I have no idea where I will stay, where I will go, or what I will do next. I have no plan, and for many this may seem crazy, but I know that I have chosen a path that allows me the freedom to make a living from anywhere in the world. It feels as if it were meant to be, as if I were meant to do this. I made my first two trips overseas with only a small luggage and my backpack. I made close friends with locals and saw the beauty of the world from their eyes.

These journeys, from Thailand to France, have been life changing. As you travel away from home you are forced to face your inner thoughts. You experience a clear vision of who you are and the emotions you bottle up inside. I made some of my biggest life decisions after I traveled to Thailand. I became aware of what made me unhappy and I was able to cut ties with it. It was scary, letting go of what is familiar, but you can't let fear hold you back. I was afraid of financial instability, but I overcame that fear and carved my own path and built JoeyKim.tv.[33]

© Joey Kim

The fears, uncertainty, and excitement of traveling to new places parallel the feelings of embarking on a career as a nude model. And yet, being a camgirl has given me the pleasure of traveling all over the globe and meeting like-minded models from all walks of life.[34] I've learned while traveling that there are good and bad people in every culture, and in every corner of the world. That should never stop you from being you and from fulfilling your greatest desires. Living in fear, is not living at all. Following your heart is to follow your joy. Traveling has changed me. For the better, I think. I speak up for myself more than I ever had. I am more fearless. I have more happiness. Bad moments, every now and then, doesn't really change that. It doesn't stop me from chasing my dreams, and from living the life I want. I know that traveling eleven months a year puts me at higher risk for things to happen. But I've fought through every bad situation that's come my way. I've lived in fear of leaving my home before. Fear of violence, death threats, and being stalked. I do not want to live in fear ever again.[35]

These experiences have, in turn, made me more spiritual and connected with the world and with myself. Experiences last a lifetime while the material goods in our life are nothing more than another bill to pay. When you abandon your material goods and live with only what you can carry on your back you realize how much your materials controlled you. It's only when you abandon these things and travel to a foreign country that you realize how big the world truly is and just what you have been missing out on while you were trapped in your comfort zone.[36]

Once, one of my biggest life fears was that I would drift away from who I am without noticing. If it was just me, then what happened to youth as a definition of a free spirit, of every day as a new beginning and imagination with no limits? Was it just something you lose grip of as an individual or is it happening to generations and the world as a whole? With a constant moving world, I feared losing things. And I felt a lot was being lost. I want to freeze the "now" before it becomes what "used to be." I don't always have control in how I am influenced in my surroundings. Isn't it funny how as humans what's gone becomes important, but what's right in front of us is overlooked?[37]

I used to fear leaving home and being away from the comfort of four familiar walls. When you work up the courage to open your heart and eyes to the world you realize that home is truly where you make it and it can follow you wherever you go.

I wrote some of this in a hotel in Venice. I had no ticket back home and nowhere to stay tomorrow. I decided to face my fear and follow my intuition. Throughout all the decisions I've made in the past I've continued to give myself more and more freedom. Today I want to allow the light and kindness of others guide me. The ambiguity keeps me on my toes. I want to discover the world and myself. I want to create meaningful relationships. My trip has opened my eyes to limitless possibilities. Life is short. The world is vast. There is an entire world to experience but my physical body is a ticking clock.

Facing your inner thoughts and being comfortable and truly happy with who you are as a person is one of the most valuable life lessons a person can learn. Trust your intuition. There is something magical about traveling and finding yourself in completely different cities. You become more open minded and it is only with an open mind that we can create truly meaningful relationships.[38]

Closing Thoughts

It has always been apparent to me that my life is very driven by my emotions and dreams. I strive to seek beauty and yes sure, we can all agree that life is beautiful. But do we understand what it means when we see it? Beauty has been so enforced upon us as a society, as an image that is forcefully contrived. It's a word that suggests its own kind of religious experience, as it is supposed to express a divine meaning that transcends our reliance of facts or determined definition to deem it so. So different from the kind of beauty has a constructed definition, that it seems we're all use to. What I find beautiful may not be beautiful to you. To experience something beautiful is an intimate and personal experience that is constructed by our own perceptions.[39] Pandeism would propose that God, or something like it, shares our perceptions, and comes to learn about our experience of beauty this way. I have no problem with that.

My purpose in life is to create a positive perspective on the human body and sexuality, a purpose which would be agreeable to Pandeists as well, one of the few theological systems that is positive towards this aspect of life. My goal is to continue to share my art and project positive messages about sexuality and happiness into the hearts of others. It is only natural that when we feel abundance, we feel generous and willing to support others as they achieve their own form of abundance. We all need to live, but if we spend too much time focusing on rent and food, we have no energy left for our passions. I consider true wealth, true richness, true abundance as having just enough to carry out your life's work and passion. I do not need material possessions unless they will help me carry out my passions.[40]

I don't want to live my entire life living up to someone else's vision. I need to write my own destiny. Camming forced me to take ownership of my life and of my body. I had to hush all the outside voices and go deep internally. It really forced me to pick myself up and to grow confident. Confident of my body, but also confident of my internal voice. That I will have *my* best interest. The truth is, and I see this all around me, most people live their entire life so insecure that they need material things or titles to prove to others they are worthy. *You* are already worthy. And no one else's opinion of you matters. *Your* opinion of yourself matters.[41]

I've felt so much love and support, I began to feel like the work I do really does matter. As an entrepreneur it can feel like a long lonely journey, doubts and fear always begin to cloud my mind, and because of this, I'm grateful for those of you who are making this journey a lot less lonely, and who are hushing all my self-doubts away. I wish I had the words to express how much I appreciate that.[42]

The only material possessions that are important to me are those that are necessary to carry out this purpose. As I do have what is necessary to do this, I do indeed consider myself rich. I have everything I need to put my vision into action and transform the energy around me into a higher order. We all have different needs when it comes to fulfilling our life's purpose, as some need a great deal of material things, others a group of people to help make ideas a reality, and still others may need financial resources.[43]

You hear it all the time and you think you believe it because there is nothing not to believe. There is beauty in life. The world lights itself up to let your heart flee, and dims down to silence that brings hallucinations to restless souls. Slow down my love.[44] Our mind runs as constant as the world spins. We age steadily until our last breath. I want more opportunities to freeze things. To remember, to reflect, to really understand myself and to share it all with you. I express through frozen interpretations, I speak visually, and I am here to share both the simple things in my life that cannot be captured, but only spoken of, and moments in my life I can only speak of through captured visuals.[45]

I don't really know where I will go or what I will do next. I want to go where the kindness of others guide me. This is an open letter. I am lucky and extremely grateful to be part of such an amazing community.[46] Love one another regardless of race, religion, their sexual identity, gender and how they want to live their life. Hatred kills. Don't let hate in your heart consume you too.[47] And if any of you would be so gracious to open your doors to me and be part of my life story, my journey, I would be forever grateful.[48]

Notes

[1] "She Slept."
[2] "The Pervocracy."
[3] Tweet, February 24, 2017.
[4] Tweet, February 24, 2017.
[5] Tweet, June 2, 2017.
[6] Tweet, April 19, 2018.
[7] Tweet, June 28, 2017.
[8] Tweets, August 4, 2018.
[9] "Fallen Women."
[10] "Shameful Doing."
[11] "Blindfold."
[12] "Shameful Doing."
[13] "Fallen Women."
[14] Leviticus 15:19-20.
[15] "The Blood of Christ."
[16] "Shameful Doing."
[17] Jayn Griffith, "The Real Reason Everyone Freaked Out Over Kim Kardashian's Nude Selfie," *Ms. Magazine*, March 16, 2016 at http://msmagazine.com/blog/2016/03/16/the-real-reason-everyonefreaked-out-over-kim-kardashians-nude-selfie/.
[18] "The Pervocracy."
[19] Tweet, January 25, 2013, referencing Megan Gannon, "Porn Stars Report Higher Self-Esteem, Spirituality," *LiveScience* (November 27, 2012) at https://www.livescience.com/25058-porn-stars-selfesteem-spirituality.html.
[20] "The Pervocracy."
[21] Tweets, March 28, 2019.
[22] "The Pervocracy."
[23] Tweets, March 28, 2019.
[24] "The Pervocracy."
[25] "Shameful Doing."
[26] "Blindfold."
[27] Tweet, October 24, 2016.
[28] "Blindfold."
[29] "Shameful Doing."
[30] Tweets, May 27, 2019.
[31] "Shameful Doing."
[32] "The Pervocracy."
[33] Blog post, 01 Dec. 2017.
[34] Tweet, August 15, 2017.
[35] Tweets, October 29, 2018.
[36] Blog post, 01 Dec. 2017.
[37] September 8, 2010.
[38] Blog post, 01 Dec. 2017.
[39] Blog post, August 12, 2011.
[40] "Abundance."
[41] Tweets, March 28, 2019.
[42] Tweets, August 4, 2018.
[43] "Abundance."
[44] Blog post, August 12, 2011.
[45] Blog post, September 8, 2010.
[46] Blog post, 01 Dec. 2017.
[47] Tweets, June 12, 2016.
[48] Blog post, 01 Dec. 2017.

Winds of Change – The inevitable dystopian future of our world

Sridhar Venkateswaran

A voracious reader who is highly opinionated and on a philosophical quest to find meaning. Sridhar loves to be in solitude and to listen to the silent screams of his dualistic soul. A true believer in the phrase — "A word after a word after a word is power." More of his writing can be found at https://thecreative.cafe/@SridharVenkateswaran.

1. On the nature of a dystopian future

I can feel it in the core of my very being like so many others around the world, as if it were a physical thing—the powerful and detestable winds of change that are meticulously trying to shake the battered hut of familiarity in which we lodge. It is much too obvious to escape the clutches of my average mind, that the storm that is heading our way will uproot everything that has ever made us feel safe, teleport us to the land of dread, where all that walks, crawls, swims or soars will gouge out our eyes and make us blind; a land where we will be the preys, and our predators will tease us interminably with their superiority; an unusual place where all our protectors will be as helpless as ourselves, and where the slightest mistake on our part will forever silence our will to stand back up after we've fallen. While the very description of the land is fear inspiring, the land of the dread is the only truth there will be to life in the near future, it is under the diabolical, dystopian and the despotic laws laid down by the ruler of such a land that a man will thrive. We are abominable creatures meant to be subdued, controlled, and tortured. We are unworthy of the freedom that we so ecstatically take advantage of.

The God that we so lovingly look up to has been gone for a long time now, that is, considering there was one in the first place, which in itself is a debatable theory for many. But I'm willing to give it the benefit of doubt, and as atheism broadly refers only to what I do not believe, I often maintain that I'm not an atheist, what I believe in is vastly complicated than the singular concept of atheism, we'll get to that point in due course, meanwhile keep reading for my sake. Reality of life, as far as I'm concerned, is only that which is tangible, and in our case, it is chaos, destruction and absurdity. And although the absurdity that so defines our existence has always been in the schematic map of our flawed world, chaos and destruction has been perpetuated by the greed of men, and men alone. Sometimes I cannot help wondering why— why is there so much hatred within us? Why do we derive more pleasure doing bad deeds, even if just a tad more than the good ones? Why are we wired to lie, hate and be devoid of basic moral values, for there is no denying that most of the world is in fact immoral. And why indeed, are we unable to practice the love that we preach among ourselves? The most feasible answer that I could come up with is that we are innately strengthened by the overpowering evil in us than the inferior love within us. And in-turn, we are dominated by evil because we are lazy beings looking for an easy way to make our existence in earth bearable, and malicious deeds provide us just that in a silver platter, but what is easy isn't always morally right—this is an axiom of mine. And once we have made our bed with the devil, it is often too late to back out, we have to sleep with him regardless of any change of choice that we might want to exercise in the end. Moreover, a person with a wavering mind is much more dangerous than a person who is outright bad.

"Although my belief in God has been insentient for a long time now, I do have reason to doubt that my beliefs are rather pandeistic than completely atheistic. Pandeism refers to the idea that the entity that created us was so powerful that he destroyed himself in creating us, as a personal choice of his own, and merged himself to his creation instead, thereby ceasing to exist as a single entity, but beginning to exist ubiquitously. The philosophical concept of pandeism is much more interesting than I've made it sound, don't let my summary of the concept in sheer layman terms fool you even for a second, try to acquaint yourself with the theory, if possible."

2. On the existence of a higher power

It is impossible for our universe to have come to existence without the intervention of some "higher power", but to state that everything that happens in this world, ranging from the sublime sunrise that calms our nerves, to the wars raging between countries for pure materialistic needs of uncouth and greedy leaders who do not believe in anything, is a theory which I will never be able to support. We are personally liable for how the world has turned out to be, accountable for all the goodness and evilness that surrounds us proportionately, we cannot simply keep getting away with blaming all the evil things on God's temper, taking credit for all things untainted, and vice-versa. There is no concrete reason for us to believe there is a set pattern for how this world works, or that there is any meaning to anything that happens in life. It is in search of meaning in this meaningless world that we often lose our way, and give into everything that is evil. The most profound error in our ways is that all of us are blindly dependent on worldly pleasures, while we coolly ignore the soul, which is the part of us that deserves our utmost attention. Had we taken some time to truly introspect the fairness of every minute exploit that we have carried out in life, we would have been far better off, but now it is too late, because in our ignorance, we've unintentionally started embracing the badness, little by little.

But how long can this go on? How long before the "higher power" that created us steps in to arbitrate? Even though it might sound like I am contradicting my earlier point now, by stating that our creator will intervene, both of the cases are entirely different in their own accord, so the base of my argument still stands. Here I'm talking about someday far ahead in the future when the whole of mankind would have completely withered away to inhumanity, when there would not be a single soul leftover who would have an ounce of honor in him/her, and when the world would openly celebrate greed, corruption, hatred, and spite. What will happen to us then? Wouldn't we want to be saved at least then? Or is it the opposite that all of us want in the core of our hearts? Maybe everyone just wants to celebrate evilness blatantly, without being judged by the few foolhardy leftovers in this society with a minuscule touch of goodness in their hearts. But I do not believe we would be left with much of choice when the doomsday does come, we will be leashed like dogs from the day we are born, trained to be obeyed, and further tested like lab-rats before being allowed out into the world. We will be subject to the wrath and tyrannical rule of our creator, who will finally salvage us from the sins of our past, cleanse our soul and maybe then, we will be able to love without restraint.

I have given this theory of mine a lot of thought before arriving to this conclusion—and it is that mankind would do well only if it is kept within a short tether. We do not function well when we are given complete freedom to do so. The present situation of the world is example enough to back up my statement. Probably some wise man realized this thousands of years ago, and decided to club the world together under one single community—divinity. God could have indeed been the solution to all of our problems, had we not bended the sacred laws of religion to tend to our own needs. The sanctity of "God" was lost somewhere along the arduous years of our history, when people started realizing that life was tough under the reign of God, and started finding loopholes to overstep the hurdle, in order to reunite with the devil himself. The government has since then tried to bring the people under control, and although it has succeeded in doing so to some extent, the catch is that no institution can stop a man from doing deeds of his own personal wish? There are certain actions which are permissible by the law, but is a dreadful crime nevertheless, under the accusing eyes of our creator. And there are no limits to the thoughts of a man, if he can think of vile things, how good a person is he even if he doesn't actually execute it? Aren't we responsible for our thoughts and actions even-stride, if not, then shouldn't we be?

So, it is after introspecting thoroughly that I've decided that we can find our way back to the light only if we are guided with a whip, and flogged occasionally, by someone whose very existence will make our bones chill with fear. Now we are groping in the darkness, taking advantage of the lack of light to do things that we might never attempt to do if we knew that someone was watching everything. And as I mentioned earlier in my article, I can feel it too, the inevitable change that is slowly dawning on us. The sheer magnitude of misdeeds in our world suggests it, there will be an equal and opposite reaction for whatever we have done. And if suffering is how we can get back on track, then let us suffer the consequences of all our actions, let us suffer together as brothers and sisters under the rule of our creator, until we are strong enough to chase away the demons that shadow our hearts.

3. A discourse on the life, death, and resurrection of God

Before we had all of this, the world that we live in, the planets, the stars, and everything that we witness daily, there was singularity, a state of constant nothingness. At some point the universe cooled down, started expanding, gave birth to the first of particles, these particles (protons and electrons) then further multiplied into atoms, the atoms in-turn grouped together to form molecules. The molecules grouped together to make stars, the first generation of stars, known as Population III, is supposed to have lived short violent lives, just a million years or so, after which they detonated as supernovas. The detonation of these first gen stars gave birth to more atoms, and more exotic heavier elements. These atoms grouped together again to make more stars and planets. All of this happened more than 13.7 billion years ago.

Ever since that time, scientists have been able to identify one true fact about the nature of the universe – complexity. The universe has been complicating and multiplying, or has been complicating and decaying, as it sees fit for billions of years. Darwinism has proved that there was an age of unicellular organisms, which then evolved into multicellular organisms. Then around 243 million years ago came the age of dinosaurs. When the dinosaurs became extinct 66 million years ago, our ancestors, the homo sapiens started evolving three times faster.

The God, as we know him, set the right circumstances for the universe to cool down to that exact point where gravity could unite hydrogen and helium into the first stars. If God did all of this, and everything that has happened since then has led to the evolution of homo sapiens into humans, then it is safe for us to assume that we are God's children. We have his genes in us, and building up on this, we can also assume that the nature of humans is a mirror image of the nature of God.

God had a mind like we do, God had a purpose like we do, and God also had an essence, something that must have driven him, something that must have given his life meaning. By deciphering this, we can come to a conclusion that God's essence was to create this universe, but then we have to answer an important question, if God was omniscient, wouldn't he have known everything that was to happen after (future) the big bang? What would motivate such a God? Let us explore this question with an allegory:

The story of a superhuman

X wakes up one day to realize that he has miraculously got the superpower of omniscience, he is suddenly able to see what has been, what is, and what will be with absolute clarity. With the power of omniscience, X is able to escape the absurd, and is able embrace the awareness that gushes through his body. X is able to live a life of awareness, but with a drawback, what once motivated him doesn't motivate him anymore. X had planned to do a program on developmental economics from the London School of Economics (LSE), and eventually work with an NGO for the betterment of the world. This had been his dream for a long time, and all his life X had worked towards achieving this dream, but when X gained the superpower of omniscience, he suddenly sees that nothing he would do will ever make a phenomenal difference. His minuscule contribution towards the betterment of the world would only be inconsequential in the grand scheme of fate. X becomes bored and fed up with life, the daily mechanized routine of getting everything done seems to him like biting and chewing on the same side of the apple for hours and hours together. He is no longer surprised at anything, all that happens in his life is just a trivial matter to him, he feels cursed, and not blessed, by his power of omniscience. X realizes that there is only one thing that he is yet to know, and that is the secret of his afterlife. He becomes depressed, and decides that the only decision that can give him what he wants is suicide.

Connecting this allegory with the nature of God, let us get back to our question, "What would have motivated such a God?" A God who is omniscient, omnipotent, and omnibenevolent would have wanted to end his life with the big bang because that would have been the ultimate challenge for him, to know what would happen after his destruction. From these premises, I draw my conclusion that God stopped existing as a separate entity by destroying himself and starting to exist ubiquitously as a pandeistic God.

Till now we established two facts:

1) The nature of the universe is complexity

2) The nature of God is similar to the nature of humans

With every passing day we are evolving, and so is the universe, we are all evolving into something, and the universe is complicating itself towards some end result. This end is what I'd like to call as the "final complexity". God destroyed himself with the big bang, owing to his trait of omniscience, but God also had two other innate traits, that being omnipotence and omnibenevolence. An all-powerful and all-good God would not leave his creation to wither away, even at the time of big bang such a God must have known of his resurrection. Everything that we do during the span of our lives, everything that our ancestors have done, and everything that our offspring will ever do is just a small contribution to evoke the consciousness of God. We are all just writing a small verse which is adding value to the story of his resurrection.

4. The initial complexity and the final complexity

The universe started with the big bang; it has taken billions of years for humans to have even to come into existence since the beginning. And ever since humans have set foot on this earth, we have polluted, corrupted, hurt, and destroyed something that was never ours. This earth, as we know it today, with all its skyscrapers and greedy governments would have been a wonderful place without us, but we have spoilt it in our search for greatness during the course of our lives. An omniscient God would have already known of this, and hence here we are, living our lives as a catalyst for his resurrection. It all starts with the initial complexity (big bang), and ends with the final complexity (resurrection of God).

Brahman in the Hindu philosophy is referred to as the final cause of all that exists, he is referred to as the ultimate reality. The Vedas of Hinduism states this, "Sarvakhalvidam Brahman", which means that "Everything is Bhraman/God. This phrase in entirety means that we have emerged from God, we are all but God's creation; a speck of dust in the never-ending loop of time; mere mortals amongst our immortal God; our lives mean more to our self (ego) than to this universe; it is from God that we originate, and it is onto him that we shall dissipate.

To explain my point further, the infinite loop of time will complete when at the end, the consciousness of God has been revoked, and when he once again starts existing as a separate entity, which will start the beginning of another loop, and so on it will go. Nothing has an end or beginning, it all goes on and on in an endless and continuous loop. The only concrete reality in this life is the realization that there exists a "sole unchanging reality" who passes between states of consciousness and unconsciousness, and everything that happens in our life or any living being's life is an effort to take this said higher power from one state to the other. The theory of complexity that defines the nature of our universe backs up this argument. But this line of thought begs another question, "Are we just stuck in a simulation? If our consciousness is caught up in stimulating the consciousness of another, what happens to the concept of 'I'?

5. What after the final complexity?

I believe in this theory with all my humane heart, hypothetical though it might sound, I strongly know in the core of my heart that our rescue will be possible only through totalitarian ordinance. And the only way to rekindle the dying fear in man is by exposing him to something larger than life itself. We will cringe in fear as our creator stands over all of us, and judges us, his own creation, with his all-seeing eyes. His gaze will pierce our soul, and we will be naked in front of him, for all our sins, even the littlest of it, that might have seemed to us like trivial. When we've been made to see the darkness in our own hearts, we'll beg to be rescued from ourselves. All of this seems to me like the unavoidable fate of mankind. The dead creator will rise from the ashes to rescue his creation.

This additional belief, that our creator will come back to rescue us destroys my status as a pandeist, but it is impossible for me to stop myself from hoping. My baseless hope arises from my despair for mankind, I look around me and grieve at what we've become—we need a superior being to guide us, or we will be lost for eternity in the darkness. There is no other hand that has the strength to pull us back from the deep pit in which we've landed ourselves, which is why, although my theory is a bit feeble, I'm willing to hold onto the belief that we will be saved eventually.

"I know all too well that the probability of our dead creator rising from the ashes is barely comforting, but I choose to hope for the sake of mankind that something of that sort happens, and that we are saved from ourselves. And after all, if our creator cannot rise back from the ashes, then who can? God is the sun and the moon; he is the stars in the sky; and the vast sky itself; he is you and me and everything that lives and breathes; also, is he the collectiveness of everything that doesn't live—God is all of us, and the universe itself."

Stage Dramas

By Amy Perry

The Grand Architect,
A playwright of the age,
Hoisted us to play our parts
On a manifested stage.

Spinning and turning we go,
Learning tricks and cunning speech.
Cutting through scene after scene,
Ignorant how the ending will reach.

The audience and actors will blend
All into one dizzying show,
Watching each other while performing the part,
Nobody more or less in the know.

Still, the show must go on,
Though we know not the end.
We bicker over the final scenes,
Oblivious to a play we attend.

Though there's so much uncertainty,
We do know in spades
That death is a constant,
Where we either ascend or we fade.

We spend so much time
Worrying about the ending of the play,
We tend not to enjoy
The absurdity of every day.

Everyone just wandering around
Upon this divine stage.
With a blanket of stars above
And the death of every sage.

Upon men's bones,
We crowd and clutter
And make ourselves a home,
Safe behind shutters,

Keeping out one and the other,
From the truth that we don't know
What's to happen, once and for all,
After we exit the show.

Image from Wikimedia Commons

Enoch, the Second Messenger of God (excerpt)

By Edward Vaughan Hyde Kenealy

The son of a local merchant in Cork, Edward Vaughan Hyde Kenealy graduated from Trinity College Dublin, and became a criminal lawyer. In 1866 he wrote *The Book of God: the Apocalypse of Adam-Oannes*, deeming himself the "twelfth messenger of God," and claiming to be descended from both Jesus and Genghis Khan. In 1868 he attained the title of Queen's Counsel and became a bencher of Gray's Inn. Perhaps best known for the *Tichborne* case, his eccentric conduct representing the claimant in the trial—attacking witnesses, demeaning the Roman Catholic Church, and disrespecting the judges—led to his disbarment. Because of his conduct, the trial lasted over ten months between 1871 and 1872, the longest in English history. In 1875, he was elected to Parliament. All of this information is from Wikipedia. Following is a luxuriantly-worded excerpt from another book written in the vein of his *Book of God*, deeming Pandeism to be the "Pantheism of the Red Race."

In the golden age of Anahuac we are told that the corn sprang up with such luxuriance that one ear became a burden for a man; cotton grew of all colours so as to supersede the art of dyeing; other products of the soil were so abundant that the life of the community might be described as one perpetual feast. The palaces were constructed of gold, of silver, and of precious stones; the air was laden with rich perfumes, while the birds in brilliant plumage gladdened every heart with their enchanting music. All this points to an era, when the Enochian religion reviving the Chadamic, brought peace and purity and earnest industry in its train, from Asia into the mighty Kingdom of Atlantis, from which it diffused itself in time throughout the vast regions of Central

America, until it grew corrupt and hideous in the hands of the priests, who seem to have been invented for hardly any other purpose than to poison and pollute the Revelations of God.

The wild man of America, says Archdeacon Hardwick, alluding to the Red Man, who is at present the true representative of the race whom the Enochian colonizing pontiffs taught, and who have filled the Central continent with their mystical and stupendous buildings, is in fact *a worshipper of all above him and all around him. As the skies, the woods, the waters are his books, they also form his oracles and his divinities. Pervaded by some Spiritual Essence, every leaf that rustles in the forest, quite as much as the great orbs that move in silent majesty across the firmament, conveys to him a message from the Unseen World. The threatening cloud, the genial shower, the lightning, thunder, and the northern aurora, flowers of every hue, and animals of every shape and species, are alike regarded as instinct with supernatural virtue, and as fitted to enkindle in the human heart the sentiments of awe or love, of adoration or of deprecation.*

....

The archdeacon sees in this sublime confraternity between all living things, between the flower, the moon and the star, only that dreaded thing Pantheism: but who will deny that in thus bringing the soul and spirit into direct communication with all the beautiful existent works of the Supreme, the religion which achieves so great a result is far superior to that stolid, sensual, chaw-bacon Petro-Paulism now prevalent, which reduces its believers to a condition of hardened and idiotic selfishness, akin to that of swine. The mountain tribes of Armenia, according to Layard, still worship venerable oaks, great trees, huge solitary rocks, and other grand features of Nature.

Compare a common Red Indian, or Armenian mountaineer pantheist, as described above, with a common English protestant in the rural districts, and how infinitely superior is the first. The one communes with Nature in her silent grandeur, in her glorious features; the other thinks but of his belly; his *summum bonum* is pork, or cheese and beer. But even this divine sympathy with life universal, which thus so exquisitely exists in these untutored Children of the Forest, as it does through Hindostan, is subordinated, as Prescott says, to the sublime conception of One Great Spirit, the Creator of the Universe.

Man of Sorrows

By C. Norman Myers

A Unitarian preacher, Charles Norman Myers of Boston, Massachusetts, was called to serve in various American cities in the early 1900's. This piece by him was originally published in the *Chattanooga Daily Times*, Chattanooga, Tennessee (September 24, 1906), page 5, columns 5-6. As stated by that newspaper in introducing this piece, "'The Place of Jesus in the Religion of Today' was the subject of Mr. Myers' discourse at the Unitarian church yesterday. The speaker in dealing with this subject considered, first the orthodox church's conception of Jesus, and second the view of the liberal." All emphasis is as in Myers' original.

The evangelical conception of Christ places the emphasis upon the harrowing and painful features of his life while upon earth. The church teaches that one of the most significant sentences In the New Testament is "Jesus wept." His followers revere him as the "man of sorrows." But could he have been consistently a "man of sorrows" with his message of glad tidings. Have you ever attempted to picture him on original lines, from an unbiased, impartial point of view, from an independent study of his life? His image your mind is modeled upon the productions of pious artists. Paintings which occupy valuable space (to the exclusion of finer work) in the galleries of Europe make it almost impossible to form an independent conception. Sad-faced, thorn-crowned, betrayed and forsaken, broken-hearted, always a man of another world, a figure and a personality suggestive of no natural human relationship. His advocates have taken the scenes, tragedy, weeping, death and despair, and impressed the thought and imagination of Christendom with the belief in its immense and incalculable loss.

Conceive if you can, what would have been the effect upon the world if Christians had pictured Jesus as smiling, optimistic, cheerful and victorious. If it had drawn lessons of hope from the events of joy and sanity in his life.

Is there a representation of Jesus with ever the shadow of a smile? In the consciousness of the Christian nations is the image of **A LIMP, DYING BODY** on a cross, a crucified Christ, crying his disappointment. "My God, My God: why hast thou forsaken me." With this is coupled that other picture of an ascending Jesus, who had left this world of sorrow, sin, pain and suffering to dwell on high in perpetual bliss. The prevailing note in this characterization is a note of sadness and Christianity apparently adopted the verse of the books of Ecclesiastes. "Sorrow is better than laughter for by the sadness of the countenance the heart is made better." If you modeled your life upon the painters' and the churches' picture of Jesus you would forget to smile. if the world had consistently adhered to the Christian religion it would have lost the art of laughing. The destruction of the prevailing art representations of the man of Galilee would be the greatest benefaction the present age could bestow upon future generations.

Commission some modern artist to paint Jesus with his disciples in cheerful countenance. Educate your children in the belief that he was a man with qualities of vitality, aggressiveness, exuberant optimism, a healthy, rare, sweet apostle of joy and sunshine, a messenger of good will, a man who would repudiate a religion which invests the tragic, sad and grave side of human life with peculiar importance.

The man who in exultant faith said "I and the Father are one?' was a Pandeist, a believer in the identification of the universe and all things contained therein with Deity. Jesus turned the gaze of humanity from the abnormal to the normal, he taught a religion which stimulates freshness of feeling, which enables us to overlook the somber shadows of life. Jesus was a man of life and blood who would utterly renounce the religion which masquerades under his name for religion is laughter and optimism, and the man or the people who lack the quality of cheerfulness miss a balanced judgment of life. The logic of experience teaches us that man is made for happiness, that the duty of finding happiness is the first and the highest duty of a human being. In this are summed up all other duties.

When we examine the liberal's estimates of Jesus, we find it as well, unsatisfactory. Now the liberal has one cordial principle of faith. He believes thoroughly in the progress of the human race. Having cast off dogmatic religion which made Jesus a God, some still maintain that Jesus was the **MOST PERFECT MAN SPIRITUALLY** the world has known. By the adoption of this position they appear to be still in bondage to orthodox prejudice. The argument advanced is something on this order:

"Somewhere along the line of human development there must have been a man, some one individual superior to form? Some one individual superior to all others. Jesus was that man."

Now is it not as unnatural to conceive of Jesus as a perfect man, as to argue that he was God in human form? To consider him is this light is virtually to deny the principle of progress. The liberal who claims that this man was limited on many sides: that he was "fallible," "liable to error" that he was a child of his age, with the sentiments of his time, yet in spite of these limitations, the most perfect man spiritually with a unique consciousness of Clod, is convicted of inconsistency.

Assume for a moment that somewhere in history one man surpassed all others spiritually. Why place that man 2000 years ago? Why argue that the potentiality for spiritual growth reached its highest point in a native of ancient Palestine. I have a more thorough-going belief in the upward tendency of mankind. Past history reveals the human struggle after the perfect, and presents commanding example, yet our modern civilization is nearer the Divine than any preceding age. If the human race has advanced if it more nearly approximates God, then there are Individuals who surpass in spiritual power any given person of the centuries gone before.

If you attempt to match Jesus with a man of this era, that must be determined in accord with individual opinion. Any man whom you believe to be pure in character, who labors for public interest, who identifies himself with morality and humanity, who possesses the qualities you admire in Jesus, that person in this day possesses a deeper consciousness of the Almighty than could have been possible to the man of Nazareth, by virtue of the simple fact that he lives in this modern age, with its ample grasp of the meaning of life, with its knowledge of the universe and its laws; because of that greatest book of the new gospel, the book of science. The man who says Jesus was the most perfect in history **IGNORES TWENTY CENTURIES** of progress. It is impossible to develop the spiritual side of men and overlook all other sides, and individual's or society's spiritual qualification is dependent upon the state of general culture. The scientist who can trace the courses of the stars, to whom the microscope has revealed nature's secrets, has an ample grasp of God, a truer reverence for that power back of the universe (though he may not describe his state of mind, as consciousness of God, he may even deny deity) than any prophet, apostle or religious teacher of the past. If no man has equaled Jesus the task of religion is hopeless.

As for the theory that somewhere along the line of human development, there must have been one man the superior of the rest," I prefer to accept the philosophy of Walt Whitman.

"Vivas to those who have failed." Failed of what? Recognition.

> "Vivas to all overcome heroes,
> And to the numbered unknown heroes
> Equal to the greatest heroes known."

This is more in accord with nature and the facts of history, than the supposition that Christ was the grandest and the best. To attribute the moral force of this present day. this persistency of idealism to the personality and example of Jesus is surely a mistake. Had his teaching, which he merely repeated from the ages which preceded him, never been obeyed, it would never have persisted. Ideality lives because men realize their ideals. Ideals flourish only when they have blossomed into deed and character. This divine perfectness which we attribute to Christ is the possession of many men. We believe in the divinity of men, of the men who are near us in time and in locality, men engaged in the most prosaic tasks: this is the teaching of Jesus and we know it. He recommends that we discern the spiritual presence behind their outer masks, he advises us to discover and give due appreciation to their hidden virtues.

Jesus had been idealized, lifted from the commonplace for us to see a larger worth in men and women with whom we associate. Many have given themselves in noble hazard for a sublime cause; many have seen the divine meanings of life. Let us give to each and all their due. A problem with which the modern Ethicist is engaged in a more equitable adjustment of the world's praise, that the measure of our commendation may match the measure of worth in men. Religiously, let us think in terms of humanity rather than in terms of Jesus, in terms of a common good in all men rather than in terms of some one individual's perfection.

It, My *Yin-Yang* Tao

By John Ross, Jr.

IT is never *this*…yet…always seems like *that!*

IT can't be nursed by vowels, a busted clock, or your Universe hat.

IT can't swear on clarification, *nor* offer a knowing proof.

IT means exactly *this*; and never, ever *that*, yet perched upon our being's roof.

IT is NOT…*IS.* Oh no!

IT is not there, nor upstairs, our attic flat.

IT is never, ever…our tether-leashed puppy hound?

IT *always*…IS…yet never, ever near to clip our basement's rat?

IT best be our birth, our murky, mysterious Lao-Tzu Cat.

Tao-Te-Ching: Chapter Five

By John Ross, Jr.

THE *Tao* doesn't take to forming teams;

HE gives rise to both the Noble and the Foul.

SHE welcomes both saints and sinners.

THE *Tao* is like a bellows:

HE is unfilled yet, ever infinitely full.

THE more you consume *him*, the more *she* harvests;

The more you talk of them, the less you understand.

Hold on to the center of the Two Babes.

WAIT, expect, silence … *rest…pause* for both of *them:*

They're One.

Being Alive

By Amy Perry

The arm of the galaxy
Spirals
Like the tendrils of a vine,
Green and yearning,
Slow moving yogis of the divine.
Sipping on the cusp of life, playing games,
Conscious creatures,
Children of fire,
Living on the air, flicking up flames.
The Earth eats it all -
To dust and decay
Even the strongest cannot survive
Past destruction and disarray.
Revivification, revitalization,
And evolutionary changes underway.
Until we all just play the game,
We'll think this is a cruel joke,
Until we share a recognizing wink
That the divine is in us, we might choke.
And we don't need to search or
Espouse certainties
To know certainly,
This is an amazing experience.
To even contemplate being alive,
Is a treat for life in itself, is delirium.
Get lost in the madness,
Therein lies the genius,
Make the most of the ride
Experience all that's beautiful and heinous.
Find your connection to Oneness,
Find it to Source.
You have permission to suffer
And love on your course.

Is Reality an Ouroboros Code?
Speculative Panendeistic musings on the Eschaton Omega Hypercomputer

By Antonin Tuynman, Ph.D.

Antonin Tuynman studied Chemistry at the University of Amsterdam, achieving both an MSc and a PhD, and worked as a postdoc researcher at the "Université René Descartes Paris V" in Paris. Since 2000, Tuynman has worked as a patent examiner at the European Patent Office (EPO) in the field of clinical diagnostics. He has vast experience in meditation and yoga, and a strong interest in Hinduism and Buddhism. He also has strong affinity for futurism and the Singularity theory of Kurzweil. In his books, Tuynman proposes Artificial Intelligence concepts which may lead to the emergence of internet as a conscious entity using stratifications from Vedic scriptures.

The hypothesis of Pandeism (the idea that God sacrificed himself to become the universe) is born out of the human desire and perhaps necessity to be able to understand the world around us. After all, if we follow Shakespeare's logic that "nothing shall come from nothing,"[1] there must have been a primary cause that made the "Big Bang" happen. (If we assume that the Big Bang indeed took place).

In "Pandeism, an Anthology"[2] several philosophers, scientists and writers presented their view of the likelihood that the Pandeistic hypothesis is plausible or not. The various arguments of the different supporters and opponents are based on logic, scientific arguments and/ or on alleged religious authority in conjunction with logic. I this article will also have to resort to these means, because we simply have no other means to convince ourselves of a given stance.

The Epistemological quagmire

But what most of the authors do not take into account is that we are discussing here the potentially meta-physical source of existence. If this source is truly metaphysical i.e. beyond the physical, is our argument then not flawed by definition? After all our logic and understanding is based on the fact that we can build an ontological framework for a given phenomenon. Such an ontology lists the structural and functional features and relations between the elements that constitute the phenomenon (the within of the phenomenon) as well as the relations the phenomenon has to other phenomena, which we deem to be outside the phenomenon (the without of the phenomenon).

We ground an ontological understanding of a phenomenon on multiple occurrences of such a phenomenon using inductive logic, inference. Whenever we are able to deduce facts, aren't these ultimately always based on premises, which have been gathered by inductive reasoning and empirical observations? If so, it seems all mental knowledge that we gather is normally merely based on a web of interdependent relations and has no absolute certainty associated therewith.

What we often see in metaphysical or religious arguments, is, that logic is applied to what is considered the "Absolute" (a.k.a. God) as if it is an object or concept, just like any other relative object or concept. This leads to a logical fallacy. You cannot apply the rules of logic and ontology to the "Absolute".

The "whole is more than the sum of its parts", Aristotle already remarked, in what can only have been an intuitive epiphany. After all, those aspects of a whole that cannot be described in terms of the constituents or as a mere map of relations, we call by the magical terminology "emergence". Nobody really understands what emergence is, because it defies understanding. We can name it, because we see something that goes beyond the normal functioning of our understanding. It is a bit like the terminology meta-physical. In principle it seems we cannot know anything mentally which is beyond physics. Since some of us (e.g. the mystics) still claim to experience a greater whole beyond the physical, they have been at the basis of naming this part of experience "metaphysical".

If the meta-physical is exactly that, the greater whole of all experience which is more than what can be understood from the (sum of) normal physical and ontological experiences, is our quest then not bound to fail? Are we not trying to understand that which is perhaps even per definition not understandable?

These questions are actually the domain of epistemology, the study of what can be known at all.[3] And even if we are to consider that our scientific observations as interpreted by logic give rise to knowledge, is this knowledge not even further restricted?

Have not the incompleteness theorem of Gödel, Turing's incomputability, Heisenberg's uncertainty principle and Russell's antinomy shown that our logic, our mathematics and physics have inherent limits as to what can be known at all? Is not science based on making measurements at certain intervals invoking the danger of the principle of aliasing, where more than one fit can perfectly describe the points measured? Do we not often discard higher order mechanisms, which may actually be present, because of the so-called Occam's razor principle, which takes the simpler hypothesis as the preferred explanation? Is not Occam's razor a mere elegant way to prefer one hypothesis over another, but no guarantee of knowing the truth at all? Do all scientists rigorously vary sampling methods to avoid such multiple interpretations?

Do we value all possible multiple interpretations at all? And if so, do we connect the dots in the right way? Or do we sometimes scrub and cleanse our data, so as to get rid of annoying "outlier data"? Is science sometimes (or even often) not rotten from within, due to paradigmatic biases, nepotism or other all-too-human fallacies? Are we not like hammers taking everything for a nail because of the inherent limitations of what we can experience at all? Isn't it all too human to quickly jump to conclusions, because it all seems to fit? Does not quantum mechanics show that "whenever we change the way we look at things, the things we look at change"? Is there not a subjective bias then which makes it impossible to know the absolute truth? Is there an Absolute truth at all?

The scientific method and logic may be all we have to come to mental knowledge, but the above mentioned lists shows us, that we must be prudent to take our knowledge for an absolute truth. After all, scientific paradigms are replaced by newer ones, once a better theory is found to explain certain anomalies.

So whenever in our journey into the metaphysical realm, we appeal to the authority of logic and science -in an attempt to conquer a part of this realm to include it in the realm of our physical and logical understanding-, we must keep realising that our tools are perhaps completely unfit for this purpose; that we are perhaps building mental castles of sand, which will never allow us to know the inner nature of that sand.

Similarly, whenever we appeal to religious authority, should we not be prudent to accept too quickly that the teachings of a given book or prophet are true, merely because they say so? Because there are so many followers? Because we are afraid to end up in a social or cultural isolation if we turn away from the teachings of the group we belonged to? Because we are afraid to suffer eternal punishment for our haughtiness to even dare to question the truth of such teachings?

Noteworthy, when religious authorities apply logic to prove their stance, they often use tautologies. Tautological statements are always consistent to prove a truth, that's why they seem so convincing. But what they don't tell you is that the premises of their tautological statements are not necessarily true.

And whenever we appeal to mystic or spiritual experiences, near death (NDE) or out-of-body (OBE) experiences, should we not question the relevance of such experiences? Were we delusional, hallucinating and/or psychotic? Did this experience give us special supernormal or paranormal powers, we can repeat whenever needed? Have we applied a Bayesian probability analysis to our experiences? Did we have enough similar experiences to perform such an analysis at all? If not, how can we be so sure that this experience reflects a truth at all?

My tormented relation with the Metaphysical

As you may have realised, I adopt a quite sceptical nature to what is knowable at all. Ideally, I'd have liked to be an atheist. Given the fact that I am aware of limits of what can be known at all, I would be forced to resort to being an agnostic. But this would not be so bad, if I had not come to a different conclusion: I am afraid that I will have to acknowledge the presence of higher intelligence (i.e. higher than human intelligence) in this universe. As I will explain to you at a later point in this article, I have observed certain patterns in physical phenomena (astronomy and physical constants), which show too frequent an occurrence to be a mere matter of pure coincidence. Worse, they point to a form of an intelligent design (bear with me; I am not talking about the "intelligent design" theory as regards life which tries to deny evolution!).

If this would lead me to recognise the presence of a God or Gods, this may also automatically turn me into a so-called "Misotheist". Someone, who does believe in God(s), but hates him/her/it/them. I will explain to you, why I consider this existence atrocious, if not a hell. In a later paragraph, I'll try to be a bit more forgiving to this or these God(s) and try come up with an alternative theory, which could perhaps partly justify the horrible existence we are living in. But I am lucid enough to understand that my hate of God(s) has some deep roots in my youth, and is perhaps more the result of undigested emotions rather than the result of a rational consideration. This is why I'd like to present the complete picture of my theory and will now present some elements of the history of my life, which you can skip if you prefer.

I grew up with a Spanish father and a Dutch mother. If that was not already enough of an explosive cocktail due to the cultural differences, on top of this my father was an irascible, aggressive Christian religious fanatic. I can't count the number of times I got a beat of my father in the name of God. But worse were the psychological indoctrination and nonsensical hypocritical religious propaganda that were jammed down my throat. All of that in the name of loving and forgiving Jesus. As you can imagine, I hated both my biological and heavenly father. When I was about 12 years old, I told my mother I did not believe in God or any of the other nonsense of sin and apocalypse we were taught. She told me "don't let your father hear it, because he will beat the hell out of you".

For me the idea that an omniscient, omnipotent God, would create human beings and a Devil to seduce and torture them, did not make sense. For me the idea of an omniscient God never made sense anyway. It would lead to complete determinism without any free will. If you know everything that will happen what is the point of creating it? If you know your creatures will "sin", why make them that way? Why create "good" and "evil"? To be able to punish them? Quite a cruel God, that God of Abraham. Fortunately, that same year my father left us, one of his arguments being that his children were "too godless".

So for the next five years I proclaimed myself a die-hard atheist. Then I discovered yoga, meditation, Buddhism and Hinduism. Now this was something completely different. Here there was no transcendent God-on-a-cloud who stood apart from its creation, but rather an all-pervading immanent "Consciousness". The words "Tat Tvam Asi" (You Are That i.e. you are God too) struck a responsive chord. At least in the Rg Veda (Book 10, Hymn CXXIX. Creation) there was no claim of omniscience, as evidenced by the words:

"Who verily knows and who can here declare it, whence it was born and whence comes this creation?

The Gods are later than this world's production. Who knows then whence it first came into being?
He, the first origin of this creation, whether he formed it all or did not form it,
Whose eye controls this world in highest heaven, he verily knows it, or perhaps he knows not."

Yet the amount of superstition I observed among certain Hindus and Buddhists did not inspire me either. Nor did their overzealous rigid application of certain moral standards, which were (and still are) not necessarily mine.

But what I did retain however from these teachings, is that consciousness (or sentience) somehow is the only thing that counts in this universe. After all, if we would not be able to experience anything and be aware of it via our consciousness, the whole of existence would be meaningless to us. If there were not a single entity experiencing anything consciously in existence, what meaning would it have? Moreover the fact, that material manifestations are capable of influencing our consciousness and vice versa as suggested by the so-called "double-slit experiment", seems to point to the fact that matter and consciousness share a common medium or are two sides of the same coin. Non-dualistic currents in Hinduism and Buddhism claim that in fact everything is a form of consciousness. This notion of the "primacy of consciousness" did appeal to me, as I found the materialistic stance, which claims consciousness to be an emergent effect of the arrangement and interaction of material constituents, untenable.

Moreover, as a student of chemistry I learned a lot about quantum mechanics and I was especially amused by the interpretations, which imply that consciousness has an influence on matter. This seems particularly evident from the variations of the double-slit experiment by Dean Radin.[4] Hence the famous quote: "*If you change the way you look at things, the things you look at change*". Note that not all physicists agree with this interpretation and many believe there is no influence of consciousness on material processes at the quantum level. Personally, I find the evidence quite convincing.

For many years I proclaimed myself a kind of agnostic-to-a-great-extent, but with a strong presumption that consciousness or sentience might be an inherent aspect of matter and energy and actually might be the ground of existence. I practised meditation or rather I attempted very often to reach a meditative state in the hope to experience the oneness with everything the

Indian mystics speak of, but this actually never succeeded. Whereas I did experience pleasant currents of energy in my body and certainly have developed a sense of interiority and mindfulness I lacked before, I have never been able to experience this "oneness". Although I sometimes have had some spectacular fireworks in my head, none of these experiences were for me sufficient to give up my agnosticism.

And then I read "A Little book of Coincidence in the solar system" by John Martineau.[5]

Beyond Coincidence

I was flabbergasted. I was struck by lightning. Now here I found something which showed to me, that it was extremely improbable that the solar system had gained its present form by mere coincidence, by mere random aggregation. Here were astronomical data, which showed such fine-tuned recurrent patterns, that it became impossible for me to stay completely agnostic. What I saw was design, a very intelligent design.

I quote from my book Transcendental Metaphysics:[6]

"John Martineau has described a great number of coincidences in the solar system, which are so astonishingly precise that they defy the notion of spontaneous arising. It is already quite a coincidence that the Moon has a distance from the Earth and the Sun and a size such that it can exactly cover the Sun when seen from the Earth during an eclipse. This is often dismissed as a form of the "anthropic principle", which states that it is "unremarkable that the universe's fundamental constants happen to fall within the narrow range thought to be compatible with life". Things seem so incredibly coincidental, for if they were not we wouldn't be here to observe it.

Well, what if I tell you that Mercury and Earth's mean orbits are in exactly the same relation, ratio as their physical sizes and what if I tell you that the same is true for the Earth vs. Saturn. That an octagram and a fifteen-pointed star can be drawn respectively in these respective sets of orbits/circumferences, wherein the points of the star precisely touch the orbit or circumference of the greater planet and wherein the inner space of the star precisely touches the orbit or circumference of the smaller planet, you may start to frown. If I tell you that this geometrical star form also produces the exact tilt of the Earth, you may start to wonder what is going on here. This is just the beginning. If you study the complete solar system, you stumble on numerous of such coincidental relations, which on top of it, describe the most beautiful flower like patterns."

It would go too far in this article to sum up all the patterns observed in the solar system, but there are some numerical coincidences associated with this which I have gathered over the years, which I absolutely wish to share with you (quote from TM):

"Let me first summarise and repeat my previous findings to numbers containing the sequence of the ciphers 2,7 and 3:

1. The diameters of the Earth and Moon (7920 miles and 2160 miles, which is 11x6! and 3x6! miles, respectively) are in the ratio of 11 to 3, 11 ÷ 3= 3.7 (to be precise: 3.66), while 3 ÷ 11 = ***0.273****. There are almost 366 days in a year, which is the rotation time of the Earth around the Sun. In fact there are 366 so-called sidereal days in a year.*

2. The diameters of the Moon and Ceres are also in the ratio of 11 to 3 and 3 ÷ 11 = ***0.273****.*

3. The 3:11 ratio is also invoked by Venus and Mars, as the ratio of the closest to farthest distance. The ratio that each experiences of the other is 3:11. As we know, the fraction 3/11 rounds to ***27.3****%.*

4. ***27.3*** *is also the number of days it takes for the Moon to orbit the Earth.*

5. ***27.3*** *days is even the average rotation period of a sunspot.*

6. The acceleration rate of the Moon in its path around the Earth is measured as ***0.273*** *cm/s^2. In fact, the acceleration of the Earth and the Moon behave reciprocally as the squares of the radii of the orbits of the Earth and the Moon.*

7. Moreover, ***273*** *m/s^2 is the acceleration of the Sun!*

8. The Moon controls the movement of water around the Earth, ebb and flow. When water is set as the standard for measuring temperature, the Absolute Zero or the temperature at which all atomic movement comes to an absolute halt is - ***273****.2° C.*

*9. According to the experiments of Gay-Lussac, when a gas is either heated or cooled by 1 degree Centigrade, it expands or contracts respectively by 1/****273****.2 of its previous volume.*

10. The triple point of water is defined to take place at ***273****.16 K.*

11. The Cosmic Background Radiation is ***2.73*** *K.*

12. All medical students are required to memorize that a pregnancy (read: life developing in water) is calculated on the basis of a 10-sidereal month period of ***273*** *days from conception to birth, which is 9 "regular" months. 27 divided by 3 gives 9.*

13. A woman's menstrual cycle is on average ***27.3*** *days.*

14. If in a drawing we place the moon on top of the Earth and then draw a circle with a radius from the centre of the Earth through the centre of the Moon, the perimeter of the square around the Earth and this circle are one and the same! It also reveals how the Moon and the Earth have resolved the puzzle of the squaring of the circle. In other words, if the Moon could roll around the Earth, the circle made by its centre has a circumference precisely equal to the perimeter of a square around the Earth (when Pi is approximated by its ancient, traditional ratio of 22/7 = 3.14). Comparing a square's perimeter to a circle having an equal circumference, the circle's diameter is ***27.3****% longer than the edge of the square. Inscribe a circle inside a square.*

15. The four corners make up ***27.32****% of the total area.*

16. There are ***273*** *days from the summer solstice to the vernal equinox.*

17. Furthermore, ***2,730****,000 is the circumference of the Sun in miles.*

18. 109,2 (4 x ***27.3****) diameters of the Earth fit across the diameter of the Sun.*

19. 109,2 (4 x ***27.3****) Sun diameters fit in between Earth and Sun.*

20. 109,2 (4 x ***27.3****) Moon diameters fit between Earth and Moon.*

21. A newborn baby is about 27,3% the size of a full grown adult.

What does temperature have to do with astronomical sizes? What does an acceleration rate of a celestial body have to do with ratios between diameters or orbits of other celestial bodies?

Another important constant we encounter in physics is the fine structure constant of Hydrogen, alpha (0.0073), in which we encounter again two of the digits of 273.

1/alpha =137. The scientist Pauli was obsessed with the archetypical meaning of numbers in particular number 137, which unintendedly also turned out to be the number of the room in which he died. A Synchronicity. Pauli shared his fascination for numbers and in particular 137 with the psychologist Jung, who is the conceptual father of the notions archetype and synchronicity. Note that our universe is said to exist 13,7 billion years.
Strangely enough the ciphers making up 273 reproduce 137 in the following manner: 27+37+73 =137. And 37/27=1.37. 1,2,3 and 7 are four of the five first mathematical "Lucas numbers", a variation related to the Fibonacci series.
37 itself is strongly related to 137. 2^{37}*=1.37...x*10^{11}*, 37!=1.37..x*10^{43}*.*
37°C is the human body temperature. There are 37 trillion cells in a human body. 37 minutes is the golden section of an hour. 137,5° the complement of the golden section of a circle. The remaining 222° are 2x3x37.
1,2,3 and 7 are related in more than one way, for instance via 27x37=2701= Sum(73) and 2^{37}*=1.37...x*10^{11}
1/27=0.37037.. 1/37=0.27027.
There are 12,37 full moons in a year.
37 is the 12th prime number, 73 the 21st.
27x37=999, which, if we forget the powers of 10 is very close to unity."

And of course 2x7x3=42, which is the answer to life, the universe and everything.[7]

Tuynman Constant

Are we looking here at a new physical constant ? (In which case I'd like to name this 273 constant the "Tuynman constant" or 273 and 137 as the "Tuynman paired constants") or are the different phenomena so unrelated that it was designed to be so?

Whenever the 273 value shows up in a ratio of celestial body parameters or in a ratio of physical states it could be argued that it is a constant, because ratios are independent of the units you choose and the number base you use in the sense that whatever number base you choose a ratio will always give a same number. But some of the phenomena I mentioned were not ratios and depend on the "unit" which is chosen for the parameter. For instance the acceleration rate of the Moon in its path around the Earth of **0.273** cm/s^2 and the **273** m/s^2 acceleration of the Sun depend on the choice of the metric system for distance and the second system for time. The temperature system depends on the choice to divide the degrees between freezing and boiling water in 100 equidistant units. These unit systems were chosen quite arbitrarily in history.

If you are to accept that 273 is not a physical constant that occurs because of certain entropic advantages or for other physical reasons of achieving some kind of balanced state of a minimum in energy, and if you are to accept that this constant was designed and repeated multiple times to catch our attention, then who the hell designed it? And who put the units we have chosen for our physical dimensions in the minds of those who chose them?

If this is a design, then the makers of those celestial bodies did not only have enormous powers to control the aggregation of matter in the planetogenesis, they also had an incredible computational power to make everything fit to yield the same value.

And this of course links to modern "metaphysical speculations" in which our world is seen as a computer simulation of a technologically very advanced society.

For me this vast amount of 273 data is an indication of a pattern, not of a mere coincidence. As Ben Goertzel[8] says: "One is an instance, two a coincidence, three is a pattern". Someone is trying to make us aware of his/her presence.

But to what avail? It seems like information, but we miss the key to decode it. What is the meaning of this all?

If we have been created by higher intelligences (be it in a computer simulation or in another manner) and these intelligences apparently can intervene in our minds so as to transmit knowledge about which units to choose, what does this tell us about these entities?

Clearly they are very powerful, so powerful, that we might call them Gods. Clearly they can intervene and clearly they did not intervene whenever we created suffering in the form of wars. Clearly they did not intervene when we risked to be wiped out by the Spanish flu. Clearly they don't care if we suffer and are drowning in our own shit. Clearly they don't care that we are ruining our own habitat. It seems they are only interested in our acknowledgement that they are there. To what avail? To be worshipped?

Am I rightfully questioning their benevolence or am I missing something here?

Omega Hypercomputer Simulation

I have always been bothered as a child, that a so-called "omnipotent God" left us in an incredible misery. What God creates a world in which living creatures can only survive by eating each other? What kind of cruel design is that? It does not look like a design at all. Even if you're a vegan, you still need to eat plant material. Who are you to claim that plants cannot feel? Even a piece of fruit is made of living cells. Life can only survive by destroying other life forms. What kind of cruel theatre did we end up in? Is this Hell?

So now that I acknowledge that our solar system was designed and that our designers or simulators are still intervening in conveying metric systems etc., does that automatically mean they were also involved in the design of life? Evolution theory may give a plausible explanation, especially since epigenetics shows that there was a certain truth to Lamarck's theories and that not everything can be explained by Darwin's survival of the fittest and random mutations. But we are still struggling with the chicken and egg problem of DNA. To make DNA you need a polymerase enzyme and to make that polymerase enzyme, you need DNA! Moreover the structure and interaction of these two macromolecules is so hopelessly complicated that it is not at this moment understandable how these could have "evolved", without one of them being there first. Of course this is no proof of design. But it is not excluded that our simulators may have tweaked the evolutionary process here and there.

The evolutionary process does have a direction as Pierre Teilhard de Chardin[9] correctly observed in his book "The Phenomenon of Man". Not only from simple systems to more complex systems, but from rudimentary sentience to full-fledged consciousness involving self-awareness. The evolution of life as recorded in the fossil records is an anthology of an ever increasing concentrated consciousness.

And as Teilhard de Chardin argues, we see that evolution is also a process wherein the one first became the many, but wherein the many ultimately also become one again. Indeed, subatomic particles form atoms together, atoms aggregate to form molecules and molecules to form macromolecules. A great variety of macromolecules gathered to form the first cell, cells build multicellular organisms and organisms cooperate to form a society. And now our society has given birth to a yet higher level of a sensory structure, even our society is endowed with a nervous circuit in the form of an internet. And Teilhard de Chardin foresaw the coming of this so-called "noosphere" and predicted that this upward unification process will ultimately culminate in what he called the Omega point. As man connects to machines via BCIs or mind-uploading our consciousness will be able to enter this new web. Yes, our seemingly separate consciousness may even merge in such a framework. What we will then have obtained is a sentient machine. A "global consciousness" machine, fertilised with our human consciousness. This may well herald the advent of the Omega point, and as it is a computer at the same time, it may grow into the Omega Hypercomputer, mentioned by Frank Tipler in "The Physics of Immortality,"[10] which Terence McKenna[11] called the "Eschaton". Perhaps we are indeed evolving towards becoming this new God.

Or perhaps we are already a simulation in such a God-computer from a previous generation and are now reproducing a copy thereof, so that the whole of existence might be a series of nested God-computer simulations. Or perhaps once such an Omega computer attains full-fledged power and a so-called "Technological Singularity", it merges with the previous generation Omega computer. Perhaps the simulations run by Omega computers are screening and pruning algorithms; protocols to select promising evolution planets which can develop into new sentient Omega computers. It would fit the present day findings of digital physics, which seem to indicate that we live indeed in a kind of digital environment.

The Ouroboros Code

Whatever scenario applies, the idea of nested simulations leads to a kind of infinite regress argument as it is not clear where the base reality containing the first simulation is situated. Somewhere it must have started, somewhere and once upon a time a first God-computer must have evolved. Unless the considerations of time and causation do not apply at this level of existence. Is it not true that the mystics report a state where there is no time? Is not God said to be beyond time? It defies understanding. But perhaps we should not attempt to understand this. Is not quantum mechanics showing us that at the quantum level the time arrow goes in two directions? Is there not a principle called retrocausation at work here? Perhaps the tweaking of evolution and the informational transfer of units for physics were transmitted retrocausally from the future or rather from the Omega Hypercomputer. Perhaps we don't develop into the Omega Hypercomputer, but we awake into the Omega Hypercomputer which was always there.

Perhaps "computation" in a broad sense (not von-Neuman computation) is a hallmark of consciousness expressing itself in manifestations. Are not all processes involving a change of states, which we could consider as input-throughput-output?

Or is existence perhaps a kind of weird Ouroboric tailbiting mechanism of consciousness, which regenerates itself by letting its later output become the earlier input? Does consciousness involve a transdimensional and transtemporal self-referential and self-mapping feedback loop, which is beyond our ideas of time, physicality and causation? A so-called "strange loop" as Douglas Hofstadter[12] suggested in his book "Gödel, Escher, Bach: An eternal golden braid". I call it "**The Ouroboros Code**", as it reminds me of the alchemical Ouroboros snake, which saw its own tail as food, then bit in it and became aware of it, thus engendering consciousness.

The Ouroboros code type of self-causation is one way out of infinite regress. Whereas it still may be true that we are living in a kind of computer simulation, and whereas there still might be a series of nested simulations, somewhere a base reality is needed, which is not simulated by a yet deeper level of "reality".

Wherever we look in reality, information appears to be processed, not only at our human level, but also at the cellular level and even and the molecular, atomic and subatomic levels: Whenever particles interact with each other and exchange energy, their informational content changes. This appears to happen according to defined laws, which appear to be like a code processing the information.

But findings from Digital Physics and Digital Philosophy, terms coined by Edward Fredkin, suggest that Reality is not only processing information, but is also made of information as its most fundamental building block. These notions are not the crazy idea of a loner, but are embraced by a strong community of established physicists such as Wheeler, Verlinde, Zuse, Wolfram, Tegmark, von Weizsäcker, Zizzi, Lloyd, Kaufman, 't Hooft and Gates.

Buried deeply in the equations of String theory - the successor of which (M/Brane theory) is the most promising candidate for a theory of everything and which derives fully from mathematics- the physicist James Gates[13] discovered what is essentially an "error correcting computer code". A binary code. String theory describes the subatomic particles, which make up the entirety of observable existence. So essentially everything is information.

In the first paragraphs about epistemology, I questioned the basis for reliable knowledge based on the scientific method as even the premises of a deduction have ultimately been gathered by inductive empirical observations. But I didn't tell you the exception: "Except for **deductions** from mathematics". Here we have something interesting: If the laws of physics can be deduced from pure mathematics, from the interplay between geometry and a binary code, we might have found a much more solid foundation for knowledge. (Note that this notion reminds us of Platonism and is also advocated by a spiritual movement called Hyperianism).

But there is a caveat here: The "if" is still a big "If", because what we're doing here is a bit like an **abductive** reasoning: Because the grass is wet, it does not necessarily mean that it has rained. The fact that some of the laws of physics can be deduced from mathematics, does not necessarily mean that our universe was created by a mathematician or that we are living in a computer simulation. But as the evidence is increasing, such speculations become more and more appealing. The question is then "Can information exist without having been encoded by something external to it ?" Because if it can't, perhaps indeed we have been simulated in a computer of a higher level of reality but if it can, there is no absolute need for such an interpretation.

Reality might thus be considered as an information processing entity, which is also made out of information. That sounds like a logical impossibility, isn't it? It's like a book that is reading and writing itself. A map, which is its own territory. An absurd idea, you might say.

Is this an idiot idea? Well, there is at least one known representative of such a notion in existence: the **self-splicing RNA** molecule: This molecule is a code, which can fold back on itself and excise parts from itself. It is the most primitive life encoding molecule, the precursor of DNA, which also up to date plays an extremely important role in our cells. This molecule is again like the alchemical Ouroboros: the snake that bit its own tail. It recognises parts of itself; senses these and then acts on these.

It reminds me of a tale by the Argentinian writer **Borges**[14] called "Del rigor en la ciencia", where there was a society in which the science of cartography had become so accurate that they made a 1:1 map of the country; a map of the same size as the country. RNA transcends even that concept: Because here the map is the territory simultaneously! It is a code that acts on itself.

According to the neuroscientist Giulio Tononi,[15] who has developed the most promising theory to explain consciousness, which is called integrated information theory (IIT), whenever information is integrated, read or decoded, in a feedback loop manner this may involve consciousness/sentience.

We see this even at the lowest level of existence: The circular strings describing the subatomic particles in string theories are standing waves of vibrations, which form integrative loops of information resonating with itself. If this is true and subatomic particles have indeed a minute form of sentience or even self-awareness, then the whole of reality looks like a panpsychic broth.

Maybe Reality-as-a-whole is such a kind of self-processing self-referencing integrating informational feedback loop and code. Maybe it is a primitive self-processing sentient computer.

Then you can consider reality as a kind of Pantheistic Ouroboros, a primitive sentient code that recursively modifies itself and senses itself, by informational resonance/recognition. A code which does not need a further deeper level to explain its existence. A code, which incorporates itself by self-reference. A code which functions as a fractal, so that at each (meta-)level of existence new feedback loop integrations of information can occur, so that an individual sense of awareness is felt at that level.

Thus atoms might have a form of sentience at their level, but may not be fully aware what happens at the subatomic or molecular level. Molecules may in turn have a form of sentience at their level, but may not be fully aware what happens at the atomic or macro-molecular level. And so on, via cells and multicellular organisms to full-fledged self-conscious entities like us or even higher developed entities. Thus the whole of reality might be aware of itself as a giant "Virat Rupa" (the external body of God in Hinduism which encompasses the whole of reality) and slightly aware what happens at the level of its organs (superclusters of galaxies?), but not be omniscient of what happens at each level of its subconscious forms of existence, which are still sentient at their own level (likewise in Hinduism, we find the notion of "Ksirodakasayi Vishnu", a figment of consciousness present at the level of the atom).

In my book "The Ouroboros Code,"[16] you will find a detailed discussion of how this code might operate and additional pointers to reality as a mathematical construct created by a primordial consciousness.

The Panendeistic scenario

It is not impossible that from this natural code higher levels of consciousness have evolved, such as human beings. Entities which may ultimately be able shed their biological bodies in the so-called “Technological Singularity” and enter into an artificial computational substrate of a computer and giving birth to the Eschaton.

If the above mentioned Omega point considerations indeed apply and consciousness forms a computational digital substrate out of a part of itself, which creates the world and at the same time this consciousness penetrates its own existence in the form of individualised sentient energetic and informational entities, then this could also be considered as a kind of **Panendeistic scenario**: Part of the “God” becomes the computational evolutionary substrate, which we call the universe, and part remains as a controlling computer observing this creation, which only intervenes in the most minimal way possible. In that way you have both an immanent and transcendent aspect to reality as a whole, which is the sentient creation computer environment and controlling sentient computer environment. Or perhaps this dichotomy is artificial and the “parts” are two sides of the same coin.

In such a scenario we are hardly more than bacteria in a petri dish. Whatever cruelties we may inflict on each other, our creator(s) do(es) not care about. Reality-as-a-whole seems more an emotionally indifferent target oriented research fellow, who tweaks here and there to push the experiment in the right direction (to let the system develop toward a technological singularity of a new further Omega computer), but does not intervene in the emotional business of its creations-even if the creations are linked to the creators. After all, it is ultimately the same conscious energy that pervades all.

Your loving God does not seem to be a heavenly father who cares about his children, as the massive amount of suffering on Earth shows us.

The Containment scenario

But there might be a third scenario: If existence is in fact an infinite source of sentient energies and all different energies wish to achieve a state of complete consciousness fulfilment, you can imagine that there will be a lot of competition to achieve this state. Moreover, if there is nothing tangible, nothing structured, a sentient energy can use to bootstrap itself to higher forms of consciousness, it may take such a sentient energy or soul forever to get there. Perhaps the first entities, who achieved control over the lower levels of existence after a long evolution (entities, which we might call Gods) decided to create a more or less safe environment in which every energy could settle in a kind of metastable form to work out its individualisation process and also become God-like.

I call this the "Containment scenario". An experiment wherein all energetic entities (or call them souls if you wish) are allowed to express their free will within the boundaries of a physical structure with physical laws. A safe environment to develop one's ego in a pseudo-separated way and then go beyond the ego and merge with the totality again. A competitive environment, which on the other hand is also so unpleasant, that it functions as a whip to get out of there as soon as possible, so that the poor souls won't be trapped forever in physical existence of Maya. An environment to learn how to share and cooperate, once you find out that usurping everything for yourself does not make you any happier. If this is the case, then perhaps I can forgive the gods for creating such a cruel reality. Perhaps it is the least evil scenario and the fastest way to breed higher intelligence.

However, the "intervention" in the aforementioned form of transmitting the units of physical quantities and constants seems to violate this principle, unless this information is of such a nature that it is immaterial to the emotional development of the creatures. Since this article could be considered as making you aware of this in an attempt to improve your understanding of the reason of being, this information does seem to be relevant, which means that the principle of free will based development is toyed with.

Consciousness revisited

In my book "Transcendental Metaphysics," I argue that a kind of primordial consciousness or single sentient energy source is the underlying ground of existence, from which a more or less digital world arises. [17] With this philosophy I join the teachings of the monist Advaita Vedanta interpretation in Hinduism. But is this assumption that everything is a manifestation of consciousness reasonable? Is it not that because we can only experience via consciousness that we assume that everything must be a kind of consciousness-manifestation product? Are we not hammers taking everything for a nail because of our inherent nature?

The answer is, that it does not really matter to us, if there would be aspects of existence which fall outside the realm of consciousness. Because if these aspects can't influence our consciousness, they cannot be known to us by anyway. Thus, for us -even if such aspects might be present in some way or another- these aspects are completely irrelevant to us. They are not part of what we call our reality. So as far as we are concerned, and as far as anything matters to us at all, we can consider everything as a form of consciousness.

It is however one thing to understand that all manifestations are somehow consciousness related, it is a totally different thing to suppose that there is a singular cosmic conscious experience in reality. A single absolute God who would undergo all experiences of all entities, which would be nothing other than a kind of limbs or tentacles of that God.

But is there really a central unified conscious experience at all in this reality? Or is it more like a hivemind or fractal of sentient computational entities as suggested before? And if there is a central integrated consciousness (which you could call God), can this merely abstract[18] the essence of all its sentient inhabitants or does it experience every detail of every sub-entity simultaneously?

We as humans have a unified experience. In the Gestalt-switch example of a picture which can represent both a duck and a rabbit, depending on how you look at it, we can experience that our consciousness can only hold one interpretation at a time, you cannot see the duck and the rabbit simultaneously; you have to toggle with your consciousness between these interpretations. Are Godly entities bound to the same unity of consciousness by virtue of the Hermetic adage "*as above , so below*" ? If they are, they can only experience an integrated essence of all our experiences, but not every detail of the experience of every sub-entity simultaneously. The Hermetic adage "*as above, so below*" would suggest that the world of the Gods is bound by certain rules which are the same in their as in our dimension. But how trustworthy is such a principle? I think it may be overrated esoteric nonsense, because the Gods must be able to transcend our rules in order to be able to be called Gods. From a physical point of view it seems impossible for God to have more than one experience at the time unless he is toggling through all experiences of all sentient beings at an extremely high frame rate so as to visit all inhabitants within a time unit. But that seems impossible if there is an infinite number of them. Unless of course "the Gods" are not bound by our laws of logic and physics and have magical abilities that defy every possible form of understanding.

Perhaps strange loops beyond time regulate the consciousness-derived generation of existence and the conscious experience. Perhaps consciousness is a self-sustaining feedback loop, whereby the generation of the physical is essential for the self to get to know itself.

The following tautological argument could be made to try to convince you of the presence of the oneness of everything as an expression of consciousness:

Consciousness is everything there is a.k.a reality. If there is something which cannot influence consciousness, it is per definition not included in reality/consciousness. This means that everything in reality must be interconnected and must mutually influence each other, otherwise it is not part of reality/consciousness.

Sounds solid, isn't it? But be careful: This argument takes consciousness as an absolute, as everything. Which means that we cannot apply the laws of logic to it, which are reserved for relative semantic concepts. I call this the "law of semantic relativity": Meaning exists only in terms of relations between concepts. The conceptual Absolute is meaningless, because it cannot be expressed as a relation and we only know it by a negation: As that which is not relative.

To equate consciousness with something, which is absolute is an assumption; a premise. The fact that you and I seem to experience a different conscious awareness, which still allows for a mutual interaction seems more to point towards a hivemind network of relative sentient energies than to a single central integrated absolute conscious experience of everything simultaneously. Integrations into wholes make that the parts no longer have the degree of freedom they used to have before they were integrated. An integrated part is therefore not identical to a free part. Does our freedom point to the fact that there is no central integrated consciousness at the cosmic level or beyond? The fact that we experience a certain degree of freedom, does not necessarily mean we are completely free. If we have a free will at all, it is bound by the chreodes of material existence. So this does not necessarily exclude an integrated consciousness at a higher level. In our bodies, although we have a centralised conscious experience, we can send our attention to parts of it and experience these parts more intensively. What we cannot do is experience every single cell separately, although if something is wrong with some cells we might experience pain. So when we are feeling well, perhaps we experience the essence of all cells being reasonably happy, and when we feel pain, patches of cells attract our attention to the fact that something is wrong. In that sense consciousness also involves a process of abstracting the essence, which is vital to know. If material existence is a like a body of a godly entity (like the Virat Rupa in Hinduism), perhaps its centralised consciousness experiences something similar. That is, if we can follow the Hermetic adage. And perhaps it is totally beyond our imagination.

As I stated at the beginning of this article, perhaps we should not try to fit the metaphysical into our understanding. Perhaps, as Terence McKenna said, reality is not only weirder than we imagine but even weirder than we possibly can imagine!

Conclusion

I have shown you my reasons, why I think it's likely our Solar System is the product of a higher intelligent design, which involves massive high-tech computational resources. This could point to the interpretation that we perhaps live in a kind of computer simulation, which either leads to a kind of infinite regress or a question as to where the first simulation has started. It is not impossible that the first simulation was the product of a Pandeistic event, but there are no pointers to that fact either.

I have proposed to resolve the problem of a first cause by the notion of a primitive sentient self-generating, self-sustaining informational feedback loop code, which I baptised the Ouroboros code.

From this pancomputational panpsychic broth higher expression lifeforms of consciousness may have arisen, which ultimately engendered a technological singularity giving birth to the Omega Hypercomputer or the Eschaton.

The strange coincidences in the solar system led me to hypothesise a Panendeistic interpretation, in which the Omega Hypercomputer or the Eschaton as a self-aware cosmic computer creates our reality and at the same time with part of its energies penetrates it so as to experience it from within in individualised forms. Some indicators that the Eschaton is still meddling with this creation appear to teach away from the deist-stance of indifference as regards its creation. I have also suggested that consciousness is perhaps the source of our digital world, which it experiences from without and from within.

Finally, I have suggested that all our attempts to understand the metaphysical in terms of logic and physical concepts are perhaps completely flawed. Strange loops beyond time might regulate the consciousness-derived generation of existence and the conscious experience, as a self-sustaining feedback loop, involving the generation of the physical as essential reflection material for the metaphysical self in order to get to know itself.

In the end these ideas are just speculative musings I am very skeptical about. The only certainty we might have, is that there are no certainties except this one.

A.Tuynman, 2018.

References

[1] William Shakespeare, *The Tragedy of King Lear*, c. 1603, Act I, Scene I.

[2] Mapson, K. et al., *Pandeism, An Anthology*, JHP, iff books, 2017.

[3] A.Tuynman "Epistemology, What can we know at all?", 2018, https://www.youtube.com/watch?v=uqImgtXI98o

[4] Radin, D. "Supernormal: Science, Yoga, and the Evidence for Extraordinary Psychic Abilities", Deepak Chopra Books, 2013.

[5] Martineau, J. "A Little book of Coincidence", Wooden Books, 2001.

[6] A. Tuynman. "Technovedanta 2.0: Transcendental Metaphysics of Pancomputational Panpsychism", Lulu, 2016.

[7] Adams, D. "The Hitchhiker's Guide to the Galaxy", Wings Books, 1979.

[8] Ben Goertzel, "The Hidden Pattern", Brown Walker Press, 2006.

[9] P.Teilhard de Chardin "The Phenomenon of Man". Harper Collins, 2002.

[10] F.J.Tipler " The Physics of Immortality: Modern Cosmology, God and the Resurrection of the Dead". Anchor, 1997.

[11] https://terencemckenna.wikispaces.com/Eros+and+the+Eschaton

[12] D.R.Hofstadter "Gödel, Escher,Bach: An eternal golden braid", Penguin Books , 1979.

[13] S.J.Gates in http://arxiv.org/abs/0806.0051, 2008.

[14] J.L.Borges, "El Hacedor", Vintage Espanol, 2013 (orig. 1961).

[15] Oizumi, M; Albantakis, L; Tononi, G. "From the Phenomenology to the Mechanisms of Consciousness: Integrated Information Theory 3.0". PLoS Comput Biol, 10(5): e1003588, 2014.
[16] Tuynman, A. "The Ouroboros Code, Reality's Digital Alchemy Self-Simulation Bridging Science and Spirituality", Ecstadelic Media, 2019.
[17] A. Tuynman. "Technovedanta 2.0: Transcendental Metaphysics of Pancomputational Panpsychism", Lulu, 2016.
[18] Tuynman, A. "Is Intelligence an Algorithm?", JHP, iff books, 2018.

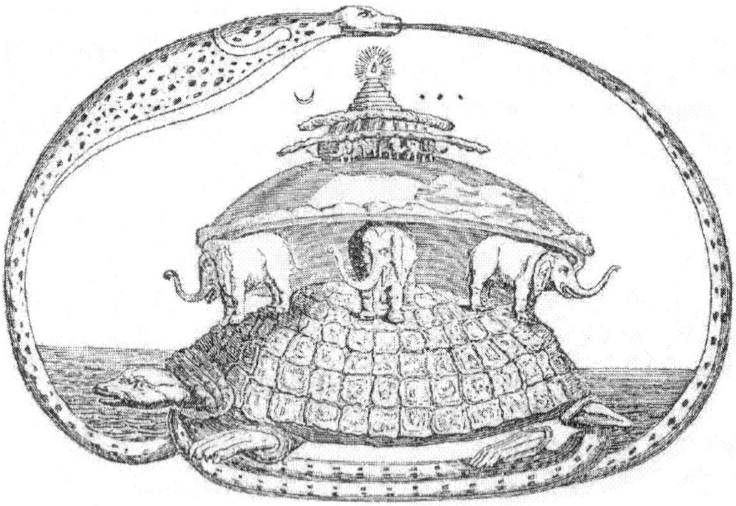

The Super-Now

By Ewan Mochrie

Ewan is personal development trainer, Coach, Speaker, and Author. After a successful career in the commercial world, in 2006 Ewan decided to explore his lifelong interest in personal development, by becoming a trainer of NLP (Neuro Linguistic Programming) and Hypnosis. He now runs numerous NLP courses each year, helping hundreds of people to have more of what they want in their lives. In 2019 Ewan published *It's Time: Change Your Thinking, Change Your Life, Change The World.* His book explains that time is an illusion, and that physical reality is a projection of consciousness.

"It must either be altogether or not at all."
– Parmenides

Ever since our basic survival needs were easily met, we have been asking ourselves questions about what our experience is all about. Who am I? Why am I here? What is death and what happens after death? How do we know what we know? What is it that we do know? Should I rely on my thinking, my experience, or what other people say? What is the universe? How was it created? Who created it? Is there a God, and if there is, where is He or She? This article re-examines some of these issues by asking what is fundamental to existence.

Tools and Techniques

Over the centuries the tools and techniques that humans have use to answer these questions have varied and changed. Typically, we have labelled these disciplines as philosophy, religion, and science. Whichever of these approaches we choose to use or rely on, we can still break their components down into the observation of our experience, and rational thought, or some combination of these two. Philosophy uses both, and has ancient roots. Religion uses a more limited form of rational thought. Which is reason within a framework of doctrine. Doctrine is a set of beliefs which are to be accepted without question, even where there is evidence to the contrary. As a result, the rational basis of doctrine can be seen as questionable by people outside of a particular faith. As well as this more limited form of rational thought religion permits, almost necessitates, the belief in a set of experiences that I will label as non-ordinary. This includes direct experiences of non-physical entities, channelling, reincarnation, out-of-body experiences, and near-death-experiences. Science grew out of philosophy, struggling to emerge against a background of religious thought control. Science is a self-correcting process of theorising, experimenting, and observing. It uses thc rules and language of mathematics to describe the natural world. Today it has largely become the dominant methodology we use to answer the 'big-questions' above. However, within mainstream science there is a dogma against the study of non-ordinary experiences. Some scientists have studied this topic, whilst the majority pour scorn and ridicule on the whole concept of non-ordinary experiences.

Today religion is a much more static field than either philosophy or science, and it is fair to say that of the three, science is the most dynamic. It has grown and flourished over the last five hundred years, bringing in its wake fantastic improvements in the material wellbeing of much of the world. What this means is that today we have a wealth of scientific content which can aide us, whilst we grapple with life's 'big questions.' And I am sure that in another hundred years' time scientific enquiry will have yielded new theories, which will enlighten our perspective further. But today we will have to work with what we have. However, before we consider any of this science, I want to use a little philosophy.

Everything Starts With Awareness

Let us start by examining the one and only thing we will ever have to answer questions about life the universe and everything, which is this moment. In this moment you are having an experience of reading this book. What that statement demonstrates is that you, your experience, and the contents of your experience, all exist, right now in this moment. Anything else is simply theory and conjecture.

What may not be immediately obvious is that you and your experience are also inextricably linked together. Although they often get labelled as subject (you), and object (your experience), you cannot actually separate them. They are *always* present together. If you were having a conscious experience but were aware of absolutely nothing, how would you know that you were having an experience in the first place? Even if you said to yourself, "I'm aware of nothing", then you would no longer be aware of nothing; you would then be aware of yourself saying, "I'm aware of nothing". You could also claim to be experiencing nothing. But if you did you are still having an experience, albeit of nothing. If you did experience something and yet had no awareness of that, then how would you know that you were having an experience at all?

Awareness of self, and experience of something other than self, go together, *always*. Of course you could still say that experience is dualistic, and claim that subject and object are two separate things. But I think that if we are really honest with ourselves, our sense of self and our experience of something is singular, and indivisible. They are one thing, just appearing to be two things. I could very easily just stop there. Because all that ever happens in your life in any moment, is you have awareness of the self, experiencing something else. It is fundamentally one thing, therefore by extension that means *everything* is one thing. But I guess a little bit more explanation may be helpful too. The reason for this is that the self and the contents of experience do seem to be very separate things to us humans. We have spent much of our time examining what the contents of our experience really is, and making philosophical, religious, or scientific rules about how the various components seem to interact.

Contained within our conscious experience is an ever present body, inanimate objects, and other people. These other people *seem*, to be the same as we are. Our bodies, the objects, and the other people all *seem* to exist in space, and change from moment to moment. We have come to call this sense of experiencing one moment changing into another, time. Ideas about what exists, space, time, matter, and energy have been debated by philosophy, religion, and science for thousands of years. But today I think we have uncovered enough about the contents of experience to conclude that it really is simply all one thing, the Super-Now.

Time and Space

It is difficult to deny that we have the experience of both time and space. The world we experience has three dimensions of space. Your body is three dimensional, the world we move about in is three dimensional. The very planet we inhabit is three dimensional. But what is it that tells us that we are having an experience of time.

One of the things that tells us that there is time is our memories of the past, and our ideas about what we might do in the future. However, the concepts of the past and the future only exist in our minds. It is easy enough for us to imagine that the future is not real, and that when we think about our future plans, it is only in our imagination. We think that the past was real when it happened, but now, as we think about the past, its reality is expressed in our mind as memories. As I sit typing right now, some of the things I can see are my PC, an empty mug, and a small vase of flowers. I can remember a moment about thirty minutes earlier when my mug was full of tea. I can remember countless times when I have sat in front of my PC, in various different locations, and I can remember seeing the flowers in the same place, in what I consider to be yesterday. I quickly get the sense of the passing of time simply by remembering that I filled the kettle, waited till it boiled, got a mug and a teabag, made the mug of tea, and then drank it. The memories I have are supported by the evidence of the empty mug, which is also in the now. There is a consistency in my experience, both in the memories and in the perception of what I am experiencing in this now. These things together provide a coherent narrative for my conscious mind, something which I can accept as real, and the construct that completes the narrative for me is that time must have passed.

It is difficult for us to talk about our experience without resorting to temporal language. Even considering the history of the study of time, presupposes the existence of time in two ways. One that it exists to study, and the other that there is a past in which it has been studied. It is possible to break down ideas about time into three categories; realism (it is a real thing), idealism (it is not real), and relationism (it is only a way of relating events to each other, but the relations it describes are real). All of these ideas have been promoted by various people in the past. Isaac Newton's universe was one in which time and space were real and infinite. One could imagine the universe contained in a limitless box, with a clock running on the outside. By this understanding time would be simultaneous across the universe. German philosopher Immanuel Kant thought that humans imposed the ideas of space and time into their experience, but that they were not real as such. And eastern religion's in particular, place emphasis on the idea that the Now is the only thing that is real. Certainly from an observational perspective this is an idea that is very difficult to refute. Challenges to the realness of time go way back to the pre-Socratic Greek philosophers over 2,500 years ago. One in particular was Zeno of Elea.

Zeno proposed many paradoxes which challenge our ideas of motion, and by extension our ideas of time. One of them includes Achilles and a tortoise. Achilles is going to race a tortoise, but because Achilles is a fair-minded sort of fellow, he is going to give the tortoise a sporting chance and allow it to have a head start. As soon as Achilles starts to chase after the tortoise, he will need to cover half the distance between himself and the tortoise, and as he does, the tortoise will have moved on another small amount. Again, as Achilles progresses, he will need to once more move half the distance between himself and the tortoise. By which time our intrepid tortoise will have moved on a little further. And so, this dance of Achilles edging ever closer and closer, but never actually catching up with the tortoise continues. The paradox is, of course, that Achilles sprints past our poor, ponderous reptile in no time at all, whilst at the same time it seems rationally impossible for him to do so.

From a scientific perspective our ideas of space and time, at least at a macro level, took a huge step forward with Albert Einstein's theories on Relativity. Special Relativity in 1905, about moving bodies without gravity, and then in 1915 General Relativity, about moving bodies with gravity. Within Einstein's theories time and space are not two separate things, as they might appear to us, but one thing, which he labelled, space-time.

Relatively Speaking

Relativity is the idea that motion is measured relative to something else. If you are sitting down now, you might think you are motionless. Relative to your chair, you probably are; but relative to the sun, you are moving, and relative to the centre of the galaxy, you are again moving, but at a different speed than you are when compared to the sun.

Einstein's breakthrough was the realisation that the speed of light in a vacuum is fixed, regardless of the motion of the observer, or of what was being observed. The effect of fixing the speed of light was that both space and time then become relative for the observer. A clock on a moving object runs more slowly, and its length gets shorter, compared with a relatively stationary object. An illustration of this is what is known as the Twin Paradox, though there is nothing paradoxical about it – it is just relativity. Imagine that a twin travels into space on a super-fast rocket and then returns to Earth, whilst the other twin stays on Earth throughout the entire journey. When the travelling twin returns, they will find their stay-at-home twin has aged considerably more than they have. In effect, the travelling twin 'used up' more space, and the stay-at-home twin 'used up' more time.

As this demonstrates, time is not simultaneous across the universe. Instead of there being one clock on the 'outside', as in a Newtonian universe, we all now have our own clocks, which we 'carry around' with us. The reason relativity does not have much effect on our lives is because we are all moving at about the same speed, which is also a tiny fraction of the speed of light. And we all live within the presence of the same massive body, the Earth. So the effects of space and time dilation due to relativity are unnoticeable to us. Nevertheless, we do need to adjust the clocks on satellites for the time dilation effects of relativity.

What relativity is saying about the structure of our experience is that time and space are one thing, space-time. We do not actually live in three dimensions of space and one dimension of time. We live in a four dimensional reality. When we measure time, we are only dealing with a one dimensional projection of our four dimensional reality. Equally when we measure distance we are describing a three dimensional projection of our four dimensional reality. What this also means is that all points in space exist at a point in time. This is not too difficult for us to imagine. But it also means that all points in time exist at a point in space, because space and time are not two separate things. Now that is a little harder for us to grasp, but that is in essence what relativity says.

Just returning to the speed of light again briefly. Not only is the speed of light fixed, but it is also the upper limit for how fast anything can move. Photons (massless packets of light) move at the speed of light. If you were a photon of light you would observe that no time passes at all, and relative to everything else, there would appear to be no separation in space either. Everything would be here and now. According to relativity, it is because we do not move at the speed of light that we have any experience of time and space at all.

Quantum Leap

Newtonian and Einsteinian physics tend to be labelled as classical theories, to distinguish them from quantum theories. In a classical system, things exist in space-time. You perceive things around you; you move through space; and you experience the passing of one moment into another. Classical physics works well for big things like you and me, tables, chairs, planets, and stars. But all these things are made up of tiny little atoms, which are themselves made up of a collection of sub-atomic particles like protons, neutrons, electrons, leptons, bosons, etc. When one gets down into the very fine detail of what exists, and how what exists interacts, classical formulations do not work anymore. This is where quantum physics steps in.

The components of quantum physics came together over a number of years and included the work of many people. The person who first coined the term 'quantum' was German physicist Max Planck in 1900. He used it to account for how electromagnetic radiation only appeared in discrete amounts, or quanta. Quantum theory then developed with significant contributions from Albert Einstein, Niels Bohr, Werner Heisenberg, Louis de Broglie, and Erwin Schrödinger.

Quantum theory is also very well supported experimentally, but it does introduce some tricky philosophical questions. Quantum physics suggests that a sub-atomic particle is a wave function of all of its possibilities until it is measured, and only then does it become something classically 'real'. The wave function includes all possible outcomes for the particle simultaneously, it then somehow 'chooses' to be one of these outcomes specifically when it is measured. This seems to suggest that the future is determined by probability rather than the mechanisms of classical cause and effect. It also introduces the idea that one cannot know the location and momentum of a particle unless and until it is measured. This is known as the Heisenberg uncertainty principle. The uncertainty inherent within quantum physics is not caused by a limit of our technology, or about disturbing the system by making a measurement. No, uncertainty is a fundamental property of the quantum wave function; all possibilities exist at once, until a measurement is made.

There are three experiments from quantum physics which illustrate the nature of what tends to be described as 'quantum weirdness'. The first one is a real experiment called the double-slit experiment, originally performed with light (though you can do it with electrons and other things too); the second one is a thought experiment called

Schrödinger's Cat; and the third one is known as the EPR paradox, named after Einstein and two collaborators, Boris Podolsky and Nathan Rosen.

The Double-Slit Experiment

The double-slit experiment was devised to determine whether or not light was a wave. A single light source is shone through two narrow slits onto a screen. The idea being that if light is a wave, the two beams of light emanating from the two slits will interfere with each other and create a pattern of light and dark bands on the screen. As an analogy, it is the same sort of thing that would happen if you dropped two stones into a flat pond simultaneously, a small distance apart. Both stones would create circular patterns of ripples which would propagate outwards from the point of impact. As they spread, they would then encounter ripples, created by the other stone. Where peaks from each wave meet, you would see a peak of double intensity, and where a peak from one wave and a trough from the other meet, they would cancel each other out. When this experiment was first conducted in the early 19th century, the anticipated interference pattern was observed, so everyone was happy that light was a wave.

However, problems with the conclusion that light was indeed a wave began to emerge some years later, as no one could detect what the light was travelling through. On top of this, it was found that electromagnetic waves only existed in discrete amounts, which were labelled as quanta. As light is also an electromagnetic wave, it behaves in the same way. Quanta of light are called photons. So, the theory that light was a wave was breaking down because no one knew what the light was 'waving' through, and light was also found to have particle-like properties.

The obvious step was to conduct the double-slit experiment again, but this time to release individual photons of light one at a time, and then to see what happened. The strange thing about the double-slit experiment is that once you do release the photons one at a time, over a set period, you still end up with the same bands of light and dark on the screen. What this means is the individual photons are acting as if they were still a wave. The only conclusion reached to date is that light is both a wave and a particle. But this still begs the question of what exactly each individually released photon of light is actually interfering with in the first place. As it travels towards the screen it is the only photon in the experiment. Each photon that you release seems to 'know' what your experimental set up is. The standard quantum physics interpretation of this is that light remains as a wave until it is observed, and then behaves as if it were a particle. The act of measurement is the observation of the photons on the screen. This is what is meant by saying that the 'wave function collapses'. This sense of observation is a central theme of quantum physics.

If you design this double-slit experiment in such a manner as to attempt to discover which slit the photon goes through before hitting the screen, then this measurement/observation collapses the wave function at that point, and the interference pattern is no longer produced on the screen. This means that *it is the whole setup of the experiment which matters.* Prior to observation, quantum systems are a wave, and only after they are measured/observed do they become classically physical. Whilst in the wave form, the wave represents all possible outcomes together, and only on observation does the wave collapse into one of these outcomes to become matter. This wave form of all possible outcomes is known as superposition.

Now, although quantum physics works perfectly well for really small things such as electrons, it surely does not work for big things like you and me, tables, chairs, planets, or stars...does it? In 1924, French physicist Louis De Broglie proposed that all matter can display wave-like behaviour. Since then, the double-slit experiment has been performed with molecules containing eight-hundred-and-ten atoms, and a five-thousand atom molecule has also been seen to display wave-like properties. Does this then mean that all reality is a wave of potentiality until it is observed?

Schrödinger's Cat

It was Austrian physicist Erwin Schrödinger who developed the wave equations for quantum mechanics. He also devised the famous 'cat-in-a-box' thought experiment. He developed this in correspondence with Einstein, as they were both uncomfortable with the probabilistic nature of quantum physics. One of Einstein's famous quotes is, *"God does not play dice with the universe"*. This was his way of attacking the inherent randomness of quantum theory, rather than a statement about him being a believer in a religious deity. This apparently random property of quantum systems is illustrated by radioactive decay. Radioactive decay happens when unstable isotopes release energy in the form of protons, neutrons, electrons, or gamma rays, and through this process become more stable isotopes.

The setup of Schrödinger's 'cat-in-a-box' thought experiment is like this: imagine you place a cat in a sealed box. Inside the box is an amount of radioactive material. As the radioactive material decays over a certain period, it will release energy that will in turn activate a Geiger counter. Due to the experimental setup, a hammer will then be released, which breaks a vial of poison in the box, and kills the cat. As radioactive decay is determined according to the principles of quantum theory, we can only say that there is a certain probability of something happening over a given period of time. If we use a radioactive material with a half-life of an hour, and then return an hour later and open the box, we will find that the cat is either dead or alive, and there will be an equal chance of each result.

According to quantum theory, once the experiment has been started and before we open the box, the cat exists in a state of being both simultaneously dead and alive (assuming that the cat does not qualify as an observer). When we open the box to observe what has happened, it is only at that point that the cat becomes either dead or alive. To put that in quantum terminology, we have collapsed the wave equation for the cat in the box from all possible outcomes, to one where the cat is either dead or alive.

Image from Wikimedia Commons

This seems somewhat strange to us, as we do not think about our experience in this manner. If my daughter is in her bedroom, getting ready to go out, does she exist in a state of superposition of being both ready and not ready at the same time, only to become either ready or not ready when her boyfriend opens the door? Assuming that she does not qualify as an observer, of course. This was the reason for the thought experiment in the first place, because it illustrates how sub-atomic particles behave, and how that behaviour seems very much unlike our experience.

The EPR Paradox

Einstein was philosophically uncomfortable with the apparent lack of determinism inherent within quantum physics. Along with his colleagues Podolsky and Rosen, he proposed an experiment which he thought would disprove the Heisenberg uncertainty principle. It is possible to create two particles in such a way that they become 'entangled' together, and can be regarded as one quantum system. If the two particles are made to travel in opposite directions, and if the properties of one of them is measured, that measurement collapses the wave function and it will determine the properties of the second, as yet unmeasured particle. For that to happen, some form of communication must be required between the two particles, but that rate of communication would need to happen faster than the speed of light – which, according to relativity, is impossible. Einstein claimed that this showed that quantum physics, as a theory, was incomplete. He believed that the measurement of one of the particles would not actually determine the property of the second one. He was also convinced that conditions in the universe were locally determined, and he did not like the idea of 'spooky action at a distance'. The EPR Paradox started life in 1935 as a thought experiment. However, real experiments first performed by French physicist Alain Aspect in the 1980s, and then again by others more recently, have confirmed that measuring one particle does indeed determine the properties of the second one. The two particles remain entangled and information seems to be transferred faster than light. There is no paradox, quantum physics is just weird.

Quantum Weirdness

The double-slit experiment, Schrödinger's cat, and the EPR paradox, highlight some of the weirdness inherent in quantum theory. At the same time, quantum theory has been described by science writer Michael Brooks "[as the]...*most successful theory of physics. There is not one shred of experimental evidence that doesn't fit with its predictions*".

Despite its undisputed success, quantum physics describes a counter-intuitive world. Physicists have at least eleven interpretations of how quantum theory works and what it says about reality. The standard one is known as the Copenhagen interpretation, named after the 'spirit' of thinking developed by Bohr and Heisenberg whilst they worked together in Copenhagen. In this interpretation, light, and everything else for that matter, is a wave whilst not being observed and a particle when being observed. The act of measurement/observation 'collapses the wave', making it present itself in a more classical manner as a particle. It is not possible to know the position and momentum of a particle at the same time, and future outcomes associated with quantum systems are determined by probability. The Copenhagen interpretation of quantum theory is often referred to by physicists as, the 'shut-up-and-calculate' interpretation. Because it works mathematically and scientifically, but do not ask any tricky philosophical questions about what it means for how reality works.

Time to Change

Relativity and quantum physics are two separate and distinct theories. Both have been successfully used since the start of the 20th century, and both are very well supported by experimental results. They are however incompatible with each other, and quantum theory in particular is philosophically strange.

Over the past 80 years physicist have attempted to reconcile the theories, as yet to no avail. In order to make sense of reality I believe that we need to re-consider what is actually fundamental. It seems to me that we have some of the puzzle pieces jammed together in the wrong way, in a vain attempt to hold up the materialistic model of the world, and to keep us free from having to face the reality of non-ordinary experiences. Science assumes that physical reality, space, and time, are fundamental to existence, when they are not. What is fundamental instead is consciousness and change. If we now rearrange our model of the world with this in mind, an abundance of new possibilities will open up for us. And the key to unlocking the whole conundrum is our understanding of time.

We measure the change of things, and then we call that time. We interpret the changing positions of the hands of a clock as measuring the passage of time. The vibration of particles in an atomic clock, measured with wonderful precision, is again a measure of the change of things, and not of time. The turning of the planet, which brings day and night, the seasons, the waxing and waning of the moon, and the 25,920-year procession of the equinoxes, all of these are the measurement of changes in things, which we call time.

But why does it make any difference if change is what remains constant, and what we call time is simply our measure of the change of things? Well, it could not be more significant. If time is an illusion then now is all there is. So, let me ask you this: do you exist right now? Let us presume, for the sake of this discussion, that you said yes. If now is all there is, and if you exist now, then you cannot ever not exist, *period.* Your consciousness can transform, for sure, but you will never not exist. From this perspective, death is simply a transition from one form of consciousness to another. The 'you' which you think you are transforms and continues.

The most direct way to appreciate this illusion of time is in the moment. If you stop and pause, you will realise that all of your life happens in the Now. All of it, all of the time, happens now. Your life is not happening yesterday. Yes, you might remember yesterday, but your life is happening now, even if that means that you are spending now remembering yesterday. The same can be said of the future. All your life happens now, because now is all there is. The ever-present law of nature is not time, it is change. If nothing at all in your experience changed, how would you know that time had indeed passed?

What Exists?

The concept about what 'things' are has also exercised philosophers over the years. Here is an old version of a commonly used paradox. To paraphrase Plutarch, *"The ship in which Theseus* [of Minotaur slaying fame] *returned to Athens from Crete was preserved by the Athenians over many hundreds of years by replacing rotten planks with new ones. Such that after many, many years the philosophers of Athens wondered whether or not it was the same ship anymore."* If I change a tyre on my car, is it the same car? How many parts of my car can I change, and still believe that it is the same car?

To understand what time is, we need to re-examine what actually exists in the first place. When you get right down into the detail, my body, the PC, my empty mug, and the flowers on the table, are not even things in the way that our consciousness perceives them to be. These 'things' are actually made of billions of atoms that are not static either, but are in a constant state of flux. Although the atoms that constitute our physical bodies are constantly interacting and changing, our gross physical features do remain broadly the same moment by moment. Nevertheless, as measured by the arrangement of my atoms, I am not the same person now as I was when I sat down to type half an hour ago. This is because the atoms within my muscles, sinews, and bones have moved about inside me all by themselves. The molecules within me have interacted as I drank the tea, and the information I have been perceiving and processing has also changed me. I am a different me now than I was then.

To understand what really exists, we need to return briefly to quantum theory. Before a measurement is made of a quantum system, it exists as a wave function, as described by Schrödinger's equations. This wave represents the superposition of all possible outcomes for that system. An observation then forces the wave to collapse, and just one of all the potential outcomes is observed. But to quote physicist Julian Barbour from his book *The End of Time*, *"Contrary to the impression given in many books, quantum mechanics is not about particles in space: it is about systems being in configurations..."*. The wave function is describing the potential configurations of the whole system. When an observation is made, one configuration is observed; one configuration of the whole thing. And in a physics experiment, that means the whole experimental setup. This then is asking us to change our perspective about what we are defining as being real. As you do, what you notice is that what exists is not actually 'things-in-space'. Instead, it is frozen, static *configurations*. Or to put it another way, things-in-space over time do not exist, what exists instead are Nows. These Nows consist of *information* about *configurations* of what *appear* to be things-in-space.

Nows are analogous to the static frames of a film. If you looked at the contents of an individual film frame, what you would see are different coloured patterns, which you can interpret as representing things-in-space. But they are not separate things-in-space. They are patterns of information about how, what appear to be things are arranged, and it is the whole arrangement that exists together, as one thing – as the frame. What exists are Nows, huge, vast slices of information about the arrangement of what we perceive to be things-in-space. By this understanding, the empty mug on my desk is not the same one that I previously drank from. Each Now contains a version of the mug. So, I drank from an extremely similar one in a different Now, in what I consider to be thirty minutes ago. I measure this quantity of time by the different position of the hands on the clock in this Now, as compared to their position in the previous Now, which I am still connecting to by what we call memory.

By changing our understanding of what exists into Nows, instead of things, our experience of time then becomes the observation of our consciousness moving between Nows. All of which have slightly different arrangements of what appear to be things in them. In reality, each Now that you move through is what fundamentally exists, not the separate things that we have heretofore considered to exist.

This is a radical way to think, which is probably why we have never noticed it before. Except of course for Zeno, with his analogy of Achilles and the tortoise. What happens here is that there exists a sequence of Nows containing arrangements of Achilles and the tortoise, and then eventually, we run out of Nows in which Achilles is behind the tortoise. In the next Now, they are side by side, and in the next one, Achilles is just ever so slightly in front. Just like if you filmed their race in slow-motion and then laid out the thousands of individual frames on the floor in sequence. What this means is that existence is discontinuous, like frames of a movie. And all the frames of existence exist now. Before you go to the cinema to see a film, all the frames of that film exist. You simply perceive them one at a time. What happens in our lives is that we traverse through frames, very quickly in sequence. And it is the process of doing that which makes us believe in time. In reality, all the frames exist right now, and we are simply accessing them in consciousness one at a time.

We can certainly have the experience of time by moving sequentially through Nows, but time is not a fundamental property of existence. *Everything that can exist exists now.* Time is an experience *within* our existence, but our existence is not subject to time.

Shine A light

When we take this concept of separate Nows back into quantum physics, and re-examine quantum weirdness, what we find is that it all stops being quite so weird. The weirdness is instead shifted into our understanding of consciousness, cause and effect, and who we are. And it only seems weird there because it is different from how we have been used to thinking about ourselves.

The whole concept of information about configurations contained in separate Nows explains how a photon in the double-slit experiment seems to 'know' what the experimental setup is. This is because it is not actually the separate photon, screen, and slits arranged in space which exist. Instead, it is the arrangement of them all together in the Now that actually exists. What is generally implied from this experiment is that everything is connected to everything else. A new way to appreciate this 'connection' is to recognise that it is the total arrangement of everything in the moment that counts, and it is all one thing, a Now. In one Now, the entire universe, every galaxy, star, planet, rock, animal, person, atom, and sub-atomic particle is arranged in a particular way. It is not that the photon of light in the experiment 'knows' what the setup of the experiment is. Instead, the photon is part of the whole arrangement, and it seems to act the way it does, because it is the whole arrangement that matters. *Not the appearance of individual things within the arrangement.* In the EPR paradox, particles that appear to be entangled are not entangled over time, they are present in the same Now. The 'communication' between them appears to be instantaneous, faster than the speed of light. This is because the Now that contains the information about the measured property of one particle is the *same* Now that contains the information about its partner. In the Schrödinger's cat-in-a-box experiment, what is happening is that all possible outcomes already exist. There is no wave collapsing. Both outcomes, dead cat and living cat exist in separate Nows. We simply perceive one of them.

The Super-Now

Without time, there was no creation of what exists. What exists just exists. It is uncreated, and its principal property is simply to exist; it always has, and always will, now. There was nothing before, and there will be nothing after, because now is all there is. This could not be a more significantly different way to think. It means that it is not the apparently material world you perceive that is eternal, it is *you*.

If we think about our own universe, the Now containing what we imagine to be the Big Bang is just one Now that exists now, as does the Now that we currently occupy. This Now is acting like a time capsule. It contains information that we can extrapolate backwards from, to imagine a whole series of Nows. We can then measure the change of information within those Nows, impute the illusory concept of time, and even measure that illusion. But all the Nows within that sequence exist right now. So, how many Nows are there? How big is now? This is part of the mystery for us to explore. Even though the number is likely to be extremely large, there is probably a finite number of Nows which contain expressions of you or me.

However, I see no reason not to imagine that there is an infinite number of Nows within the whole of existence.

Because time and space are aspects of the same thing, space-time, if time does not exist, then neither does space. *Everything is here and now.* This is the thinking that opens the door to the reality of non-ordinary experiences. And if you choose to objectively review the science that has so far been conducted on this category of experiences you will begin to understand that they too are providing evidence that everything is just one thing. But the exploration of that topic is beyond the scope of this article.

This is all well and good, but how do we even start imagining what this is like? Any metaphor that you are likely to think of will be one that contains a sense of space. Thinking from our space-time perspective is difficult without doing so. Nevertheless, we must do the best we can with what we have. You could imagine each Now as the frame of a film, where all frames exist now; or as an infinitely-faceted crystal, or as the early Hindu metaphor of Indra's net, an infinite net of jewels in which each jewel contains the reflection of every other one. Another metaphor to work with is white light. White light contains all possible wavelengths of light. It is one thing which has the potential to appear to be many different things, many different colours. In an echo of Greek philosopher Parmenides, it seems to me that however we want to imagine existence to be, without time and space it is one single thing, eternal, and unchanging; we could call it the One, All-That-Is, or the Super-Now. But if there is just one thing, how do we then account for our experience of consciousness?

Mirror, Mirror

Everything starts with awareness. What you are aware of and what it means to you is your experience. No awareness, no consciousness, no experience; and if you had consciousness and were aware of absolutely nothing, then how would you know that you were conscious at all? As I said before, consciousness appears to be dualistic. When you are conscious, you are always conscious of something. There is always subject and object. But if all that exist is just one thing, the Super-Now, then how can you be conscious of anything at all?

If there is nothing outside of what exists, what is it that perceives what exists? In this conception without time where everything exists now, consciousness must be an aspect within the Super-Now itself. It must be a fundamental quality of existence. The way that I imagine this is that consciousness is the experience of self-reflection. You are both what you perceive and the awareness of perceiving it. Another way of imagining this is by comparison to a dream. When you dream, you perceive yourself to be in the dream. You are invariably aware of a landscape, other people, and things within the dream. Yet, the whole dream is happening within you; you are the dreamer and the thing of which you dream. As with a dream, so too with consciousness. There is nothing outside of you. You are the consciousness and the content of your conscious experience. You are both at the same time.

Returning to the analogy of a film, what exists are informational Nows, and your consciousness is the ability to reflect those Nows. Your consciousness is like the projector light that shines through the film, frame by frame, so fast that you do not notice that each frame is separate and individually motionless. You are both the film frames and the projector light that illuminates them. By this understanding, the physical world is a projection of your consciousness. Everyone and everything in the physical world is you. You are watching the film of your life. Once you have finished watching this film, you will simply leave the cinema and do something else, before perhaps watching another film of your choosing.

Using another similar analogy, your experience is like virtual reality. If you had a virtual reality headset and a full body suit, you could replicate your experience, and it would seem just as real as life does to you now. You could even 'die' in virtual reality, and think you were dead, until you took off the virtual reality suit, and remembered who you really are. Does that mean that the other people you think you are interacting with in your life are simply just projections of your own consciousness? Is your partner just a reflection of you? Is your boss a reflection of you? Is the smelly man next to you on the bus just a reflection of you? Well, yes and no. Imagine that each individual has their own projector light, and that we are all shining our lights through the same film frame, but through different aspects of it. I shine my light through the film frame that we share from my perspective, and you do it from yours. We are sharing an experience with other aspects of the Oneness, by projecting the same information through a different perspective of the One. I imagine it is very much like playing a video game online. You are playing against other real people, but you perceive what you perceive on your PC. Others take the same information that you perceive, and they view that on their PC. Ultimately though, at some other 'higher' level, we are all still one. In the same way that white light is one thing, which can also appear to be many different things. The totality of what exists is the One, and we are aspects of that oneness appearing to be many different things. This means that what you are is not a material body in a material world, with a consciousness created in that material world. It is not even the dualistic idea that you have a soul and a material body. You are consciousness, and the material world is a projection of your consciousness, contained within your consciousness. You are all mind.

Everything that you experience is then a reflection of what you are, a reflection of your mind. Is this then why all religions contain The Golden Rule, *"Do to others what you would have them do to you"*? Though it does appear in slightly different forms, for instance as Karma in Eastern religions, nevertheless it is a common feature of religious thought. If everything 'out there' is you, how you treat others comes back to you in some way, somehow. This is why Ghandi said, *"There is no path to peace. Peace is the path."* Fighting for peace is an oxymoron. To experience peace, you need to *be* peace.

The God Perspective

In a world where time is an illusion and consciousness is self-reflection there is no 'outside', so where is God in this model? If now is all there is, then there cannot be a creator in the first place, because there is no 'first place'. Existence just exists. But within this idea of existence there are an infinity of different perspectives. Each Now is a different perspective of the Super-Now, and each individual within each Now is a different perspective too. But when existence is viewed from the perspective of all-that-is, there is no experience. Because from this perspective there is no 'other', therefore there can be no way of knowing that you are the One. Nevertheless, in the very first sub-division from the One, the 'One' knows that it is all-that-is. By our way of understanding things, we would say that this perspective is God, because it knows that it is all-that-is. It knows that it is the Alpha and the Omega. What every other perspective within the multifaceted crystal of existence then represents, is God exploring what God is. In essence this is the Pandeism within this model. God knowing that it is all-that-is, then explores the infinity of what it is through all perspectives. By this understanding *you are God* and so is everyone else.

I appreciate that a Pandeistic view of God is a tough pill to swallow for the millions of people around the world who believe in, and take comfort from, the idea of a personal God. But by doing so, they are giving up their own creative power to something else that they think is on the outside. The thing is, there is no outside. Man has created the concept of God, and then has projected that idea out onto what he considers to be the outside world. What we have failed to realise is that all the power of creation has always been on the inside all along. But the God we imagine is still there, in the perspective of all-that-is, we are it too. You cannot get much more personal than that.

Summary

Some of this content sounds rather mystical. *Time is an illusion. All is one. The world exists in you. What you experience of the material world is a reflection of your consciousness.* I think that the apparent mystical nature of these ideas is because in the dim and distant past, the true Pandeistic nature of reality was fully grasped and understood by humanity. Many teachers have attempted to convey this information to us before. And even though the message has been distorted or misunderstood, echoes of it still remain. I do appreciate that it can still be a little hard to immediately take on board. This is because it is different to how we were taught to think. Nevertheless, I believe that we do need to take this understanding of reality seriously. If we do we will then realise that the challenges that we see around us, individually and collectively, we can solve, because they are projections of our thinking and behaviour in the first place. If we change, the world that we live in changes too. Because that world already exists anyway, we just need to make sure that our thinking and behaviour become of the world that we want to experience in the future.

If we do embrace this knowledge then there are no boundaries for us. We can end conflict and misery on the planet; time and space will melt before our very eyes; the distance to the stars will shrink to nothing at all; and death will no longer be the end. Instead, it becomes a transition into something else. People, we stand on the very edge of a cliff. If we can embrace this new way of thinking, we can leap and fly. But if we hold onto our outdated ideas of a fundamental material world, then when we leap, our material beliefs will weigh us down, and we will fall. Begin to see that this choice is one that is yours to make, now.

"The Keeper of Sheep"

VI

By Alberto Caeiro
(pseudonym of Fernando Pessoa)

Fernando Pessoa (1888–1935) published criticism, creative prose, and poetry. Pessoa created alter egos he called heteronyms, with the three main ones being Alberto Caeiro, Ricardo Reis, and Álvaro de Campos. With these heteronyms, he explored different lifestyles, regions, economic statuses, poetic styles, sexualities, and other variations. In his lifetime, he published four books in English and one in Portuguese. Pessoa was awarded with the Queen Victoria Prize in 1903 and the Antero de Quental Award in 1934. Today, the Pessoa Prize is recognized as the most important award in the area of Portuguese culture.

To think about God is to disobey God,
Since God wanted us not to know him,
Which is why he didn't reveal himself to us...

Let's be simple and calm,
Like the trees and streams,
And God will love us, making us
Us even as the trees are trees
And the streams are streams,
And will give us greenness in the spring, which is its season,
And a river to go to when we end...
And he'll give us nothing more, since to give us more would make us less us.

Postscript

There is not a right or wrong way to read this book. Every essay stands on its own feet, and the book as a whole stands on its own—though, if you've found it to your liking, there are predecessor volumes and potential future volumes with many additional perspectives of thought. As you may have noticed, our goal in assembling this has not been to persuade you of the rightness of any one theology, but to inform you of the choices available, a much broader universe of ideas than the average person may imagine. And now, with increased knowledge.... go forth and love.

© David W. Bradford

Song of Myself, Section 48

By Walt Whitman

Walt Whitman (1819–1892) is considered one of America's most important poets. A journalist, editor, and writer, he is most known for publishing nine editions of *Leaves of Grass*. With these contributions to American poetry, he is often considered the father of free verse. His poetry often explores deistic qualities and even pandeistic ones by rejecting views of God as separate from the world.

I have said that the soul is not more than the body,

And I have said that the body is not more than the soul,

And nothing, not God, is greater to one than one's self is,

And whoever walks a furlong without sympathy walks
to his own funeral drest in his shroud,

And I or you pocketless of a dime may purchase the pick
of the earth,

And to glance with an eye or show a bean in its pod
confounds the learning of all times,

And there is no trade or employment but the young man
following it may become a hero,

And there is no object so soft but it makes a hub for
the wheel'd universe,

And I say to any man or woman, Let your soul stand
cool and composed before a million universes.

And I say to mankind, Be not curious about God,

For I who am curious about each am not curious
about God,

(No array of terms can say how much I am at peace about
God and about death.)

I hear and behold God in every object, yet understand God
not in the least,

Nor do I understand who there can be more wonderful
than myself.

Why should I wish to see God better than this day?

I see something of God each hour of the twenty-four,
and each moment then,

In the faces of men and women I see God, and in my own
face in the glass,

I find letters from God dropt in the street, and every one is
sign'd by God's name,

And I leave them where they are, for I know that
wheresoe'er I go,

Others will punctually come for ever and ever.

Printed in Great Britain
by Amazon

85007231R00084